Contents

Introduction 5

Chapter 1   The Puppy Days 9

Chapter 2   The Adolescent Dog 19

Chapter 3   Feeding and Exercise......................... 29

Chapter 4   Doggy First Aid 37

Chapter 5   Dangerous Foods for Dogs 45

Chapter 6   Fleas and Other Nasties 53

Chapter 7   Travelling With Your Dog 61

Chapter 8   Your Dog and The Law 69

Chapter 9   Pet Insurance.................................... 79

Chapter 10   Special Needs Dogs 87

Chapter 11   Adopting a Dog................................ 95

Help List   103

Book List   111

Introduction

By becoming a proud dog owner you have made the right choice. They don't call dogs a man's best friend without good reason and you now have a friend for life. Dogs are good for your health and that's a proven fact! They encourage you to take exercise and in doing so you will meet other dog owners and extend your social circles. It's also scientifically proven that dog owners are less stressed, probably because of the comfort they get from their pet: no matter what kind of day you've had, there will always be your bundle of furriness to greet you with a wagging tail and bright eyes.

But owning a dog can sometimes be a bewildering experience. There are so many decisions you need to make, especially in light of modern technology: for instance, is microchipping safe? Dog charities certainly believe it is and that's why they recommend that every person gets their dog chipped so pets can be tracked down if they ever go missing. Worldwide there's a stray dog problem, not because owners have dumped their dogs, but because there is no way of tracing them back to their owners once they get lost. Microchipping your pet will mean if they go 'walkabout', there's a good chance you will get them back.

Vaccinations are expensive and can really add to the cost of owning a pet, but are they essential? In a word, yes. In chapter 1 it will be explained exactly what each vaccination is for and what they prevent. Ensuring your pet's jabs are up to date could save their life.

Pet insurance can also be confusing. How does it work and is it really worth it? Insurance won't cover your dog's vaccinations or any pre-existing health conditions, like a skin infection for example, but it will cover you for the cost of a major operation. Think about whether you will be able to afford those unexpected vet bills if and when they arise.

More and more dogs are overweight these days, so what do you feed your pooch? How do you know if your dog is getting too fat and what do you do about it? Having a regular feeding regime can help. As can not feeding your pooch scraps off the table (it's difficult I know, but you need to watch his waistline because he won't).

And what about exercise – is your dog getting enough walks and how can you tell? What other activities can you engage in with your dog that will get their heart pumping and give them the exercise needed? These aspects of caring for your dog will be discussed.

It can be confusing to know what things are safe to feed your pooch. For instance, is chocolate really as dangerous as they make out? In short, yes it is – it can kill dogs because of a chemical it contains, but it's not the only human food that can harm your dog. There are some other doggy no-nos, like grapes and caffeine that you should also be aware of. Preventing your dog from eating human food can be difficult, especially if you have children around, so it is vital you explain to any children that are close with your dog that animals are not to eat certain things under any circumstances.

Canine health matters can also be complicated. What medications does your pet need on a regular basis (it's not just puppies that need jabs), when do they need worming and what about the hidden nasties your dog might bring home? How do you get rid of things like fleas and ticks and pest-proof your home? And what if your dog cuts or strains their paw – what can you do before you visit the vet?

This is where having a first aid kit comes in handy. Do you know, for instance, that you can buy doggy boots that will protect cut paws? As anyone who's ever tried to put a bandage on a reluctant dog will tell you, it rarely works. Usually you'll wake up in the morning to find it's been chewed off and your dog has subsequently licked away at the paw, making it worse.

This book contains all the information you'll ever want and need to know about caring for your dog, so that you and your dog can enjoy a happy life together confident that you can look after one another.

Whenever I think of all my happy memories, I think of my dogs. I hope you will too!

Dedication

This book is dedicated to Vic Pup, the bravest dog I've ever met. He suffered from epilepsy, but always managed to enjoy life to the full. I was lucky enough to spend nine years with him and I wish it could have been forever.

Disclaimer

The advice given in this book is for guidance only. For medical and behavioural advice, please consult your vet or canine behaviourist. Books mentioned in the text are in no way endorsed by the author or the publisher.

Chapter One

The Puppy Days

Having a cute bundle of fluffiness in your life can be fun, but there are practical considerations too. Puppies need a lot of time, care and exercise. They also need to be socialised to prevent nervousness or bad behaviour when meeting other dogs.

First things first, when you bring your puppy home you need to make sure your house has been puppy-proofed!

Puppy-proofing your home

Puppies eat everything and are in to everything, which is why you'll need to keep anything they can chew out of their way.

- Keep all electrical cables away from your puppy, as they will have a tendency to chew things. You can try taping cables to the wall with strong masking tape or invest in a cable tidy to prevent chewing.

- Don't leave small items lying around, like jewellery, buttons, pens, coins, pins, needles, screws and marbles, as a puppy is liable to try to swallow them.

- Avoid leaving food out on tables and counter tops within your puppy's reach as it will get stolen. This is until your puppy learns that 'no' means no.

- Lock away any cleaning products and medications that can harm dogs. Puppies are great chewers and even if things are in strong containers, they may be able to bite through.

- Get a child gate to stop your puppy going into areas of the home that are dangerous.

- Warn your children about the dangers of leaving chocolate lying around. This can kill a fully grown dog, never mind a puppy.

- If you have a garden, make sure it's adequately fenced. Remember, some puppies can jump quite high.

- Remove all heavy objects that can be knocked over. You don't want your puppy to end up with concussion.

- Remove all rugs, especially ones with tassels as they're irresistible to puppies!

Making your puppy feel at home

Imagine your first night in a house with people you don't know and unfamiliar surroundings, now think about how your puppy will feel. Making sure your furry friend settles in is vital in the early days. Too many puppies are given away because their new owners can't cope, so try to make your puppy as comfortable and calm as possible.

Give your puppy their own territory

The most important thing for any dog is to know that they have a place that is theirs and only theirs. Set aside an area in your home that's their own domain where they will sleep. Mark it by placing the dog bed there (a chew-proof one of course) and putting down some toys. Encourage your puppy to sit on it and when they do say 'good boy' or 'good girl' and reward with a small treat. Get up and walk away telling your puppy to 'stay' and if they do, reward with another small treat. This is called positive reinforcement.

Meeting the family

When you introduce your new puppy to the family make sure that the room is not overcrowded. Get each member of your family to crouch down to puppy-level to gently introduce themselves, this can be with stroking, holding your hand out so they can sniff or just waiting for the puppy to come over. It's important if you have children, especially younger ones, that you teach them not to approach your puppy from behind, or pull their tail as this will scare the puppy. Another thing to explain is that children should not approach your dog when eating, and also not to poke, prod, grab or lift them.

Separation anxiety

Your puppy may suffer from separation anxiety because they're no longer with their mother and siblings. Make a fuss of them to reassure them that they're safe. You may find that a DAPS collar helps – DAP stands for dog appeasement pheromone and is meant to imitate the scent of the mother dog. As well as a collar this also comes in a diffuser spray. Some people find this works whilst others do not, Dogs Trust currently put these collars on their dogs when they go to new homes.

Initially, your puppy will follow you around, this is normal, but you need to get them used to not being in the same room as you, if you don't they may start to cry or bark when left on their own. To do this you can use a child gate and leave the door open, so that although they can see you they can't follow you. Do this for a few days, extending the amount of time you are away from them on each occasion. Then progress to leaving them alone in a room with a toy for a few minutes and closing the door. Don't make a big fuss when you leave, if you do it makes it more of a big deal than it actually is.

Tip

To discourage separation anxiety, don't continually make a fuss of your puppy every time you see them – this means no eye contact and no praise. This helps them to get used to the fact that you have other things to do and won't always make a fuss and give attention.

Food for puppies

Younger dogs have different requirements to older ones. Believe it or not, they grow at 20 times the rate of older dogs and need a special diet to cope with that. Puppies should get fed four times a day until they are about four months old. Then cut it to three meals until six months old. After that, feed twice daily, which is the routine throughout an adult dog's life. Always have a fresh bowl of water for your dog, but it's better if you take leftover dog food away after 20 minutes, this should be thrown away as food should always be fresh.

> **Tip**
>
> Try not to vary what you feed your puppy as any change may result in diarrhoea – puppies have delicate tummies at this stage. If you must change their diet, introduce the new food gradually adding a small amount to the usual food at a time.

Toys

'Don't give your puppy too many toys at one time. This will confuse him about which things are his and which are yours.'

When puppies chew furniture and shoes, it's often because they need to keep their jaws occupied with something, especially when they are teething. That's why you need to get some suitable toys to make chewing constructive and not destructive. There is a wide variety of toys specifically aimed at puppies out there. These include:

- Tug toys (for example, chocolate-flavoured ropes).
- Chews (ones that crumble when bitten are best).
- Nylabones (the puppy version).
- Doggy Frisbees.
- Activity balls.
- Soft toys (avoid ones with glass eyes).
- A ball on a rope.

> **Tip**
>
> If you can't afford to buy new toys, why not make your own? An old tennis ball tied in a sock makes a great toy for a puppy. Alternatively, you may find toys that people have donated in charity shops.

Teething

At four to five months old your puppy will start to lose their baby teeth and you will start to find them around the house – sometimes in the most unusual of places! By the age of seven months your puppy should have an adult set of teeth.

This can be a trying time, not just for your puppy but you too, so here's some tips on how to cope:

- During this time your dog may 'mouth' you or even bite you when you are playing. If this happens don't hit or shout at your dog. Just stop playing and say in a high-pitched squeak 'no'. Soon your dog will start to learn that if they nip or bite you the fun will stop. This is also teaching that it's not okay to bite people, which is a valuable lesson as your dog gets older and grows adult teeth.

- During this time your dog's compulsion to chew will be overwhelming. To stop them chewing things get some special toys for teething dogs. One of the best is a Kong toy made especially for teething puppies.

- Carrots are low in calories and can be put in the fridge or rinsed under a cold tap to help give some relief from the pain. Rope toys can also be wetted or frozen to help cool your dog's mouth down.

- Keep cuddly toys out of your dog's way, they will be far too tempting!

- If you think it will help, you can brush your dog's teeth. Make sure you use a soft toothbrush (a doggy one has a much longer handle) and toothpaste aimed at dogs.

Toilet training

This phrase strikes fear into puppy owners, of all the things you will have to do with your puppy, this may be the most difficult. Never fear though, with patience and effort all puppies will eventually be toilet trained.

- It's never too early to start toilet training. It should begin the day you bring your puppy home.

- After a puppy has eaten, had a drink or woken up always take them outside. Give praise when they do their business and ignore them when they don't. The message will soon get through. A touch of bribery may be useful here and you could give a little bit of a dog treat as well as a pat when the call of nature is answered.

- At all other times, be aware of the signs that your puppy needs the loo. Puppies who are about to go will look around anxiously, often pacing the floor and going round in circles. They may also start looking in corners for a suitable place to go. Be watchful and you will avoid accidents and nasty surprises later.

- Try to take your puppy to the same place to go to the toilet. Their scent will have marked it and they're more likely to do their business there.

- Put newspaper or training mats (which are like big nappies) down on the floor of your home. When your puppy goes to the toilet on the newspaper or mat give them praise, if they go elsewhere try to ignore them. Puppies love praise.

- Keep moving the newspaper nearer the door and then eventually into the garden. Puppies are attracted to their own scent.

- Make sure you take your puppy out at regular times and never scold them if you find they have been to the toilet somewhere they shouldn't have. They won't know what you are scolding them for.

- Make sure you clean up any mess and use a special carpet cleaner to get rid of the smell. Even if you can't smell it, your puppy can and it will encourage them to continue using that spot.

Tip

Training mats are available from vets and pet shops. They have a scent on them that makes a puppy want to go to the toilet there. Some owners also swear by pee posts, which are impregnated with pheromones that attract dogs.

How to avoid accidents

Puppies are like babies and they need the toilet several times a day. It isn't until they get older that they can control their bladders. To avoid accidents you should:

- Take them out first thing in the morning (as early as you can) and last thing at night (as late as possible).
- Take them out whenever they have eaten or drunk anything.
- Take them out after they've become excited, say there's been a new visitor to your house. Excited puppies feel the urge to go to the toilet.

Training your puppy

This can seem like an arduous task, but don't fear, it can be done. Every well-behaved dog you see was once a puppy and their owners had to go through the training process.

Getting your dog to obey you

If you want your dog to obey your commands then you need to be consistent with the words you use. You can't tell a dog to 'stay' one moment and then change it to 'don't move' the next, this will be confusing for your dog. One word is better than a few, so use 'sit' rather than 'sit down' and 'no' rather than 'don't do that', and use 'down' rather than 'get down from there.'

Try not to shout because this may make your dog scared rather than obedient, or they may get confused or even excited and carry on with what they're doing because they think it's a game. Remain patient and keep your voice clear and firm.

Getting your dog to come back

This is the most important command your dog should know. If they don't come back to you they could get run over or cause an accident. In order to teach this command, you should start doing it in your home. Call your dog's name and when they come reward with a treat. Do this randomly during the day.

Eventually, go outdoors in an enclosed area and try it there, this time putting your puppy on a short leash. Once they master that use a longer leash. Each time they come back to you, reward with a small bit of the treat.

Don't punish your dog or shout if they don't come. Good training is all about positive associations.

Visiting the vet

Now you've got your puppy home and settled in, it's time to think about their health.

Puppy farms

'Battery farming of dogs is an appalling practice, abhorrent to all decent members of society.'
Clarissa Baldwin, chief executive of Dogs Trust.

If you bought your puppy from a puppy farm, or think you may have, you should take them for a check-up with the vet as soon as possible. Dogs Trust launched a campaign with the slogan 'Stop the battery farming of dogs' because they were so concerned about the health of the dogs from these farms. Many dog owners unwittingly bought dogs from these farms when they purchased them through newspaper or Internet ads, pet shops and superstores.

Vaccinations

The first vaccinations are called primary vaccinations. The first one is given when a puppy is eight weeks old. This covers your puppy for five different diseases –

parvovirus (a dysentery type disease), distemper (one of the oldest dog diseases that's believed to be found everywhere in the UK), hepatitis (a disease that attacks the liver and can kill rapidly), leptospirosis (a bacterial infection that affects pets and humans) and parainfluenza (a respiratory disease that has been linked to kennel cough).

The second injection is needed two to four weeks later. It's only a week after the second vaccination that your dog can go out and socialise with other dogs. After the first injection it's only safe for him to come into contact with other vaccinated dogs. The two vaccinations together will cost between £20-£60 depending on your vet.

Booster vaccinations, which immunise your dog against the five different diseases already mentioned, are given when your dog is one year old and from then on it's recommended they have them every year. This will cost you around £30, although prices can vary depending on where you live.

Until your puppy has had the full set of vaccinations they should be confined to your home and garden. If you do go out, you should carry your puppy, limit contact with other dogs and not let them down on the ground, just in case they pick something up.

Worms

Puppies have worms when they are born and are usually wormed from three weeks old. You must carry on with that and ask your vet for advice on how and when to do it. Usually, all that's required is a tablet given with your dog's food. Often worms will come out when your dog does a number two (they'll look like grains of rice). If your puppy isn't wormed it can make them have sickness and diarrhoea and in severe cases cause death.

What else will the vet do?

The vet will check your dog's overall health, including teeth, coat and heart. Your puppy may also be weighed. Vets will try to make this first visit a positive experience for your dog, to avoid stress on subsequent visits.

Summing Up

- Before you bring your puppy home you'll need to puppy-proof your house to keep your new friend and your home safe!

- It's important that your puppy doesn't become too reliant on you, or he'll suffer from separation anxiety.

- Toilet training can be difficult, but remember everyone who's ever had a puppy did this and you can too.

- Primary vaccinations for puppies are vital if you are to keep him happy and healthy. Puppies need two injections – one at eight weeks old and the other two to four weeks later.

- Puppies can be hard work, but as long as you make them feel at home and safe and make sure their physical and mental needs are met, you will have one happy puppy.

Chapter Two

The Adolescent Dog

Once your puppy starts to grow you'll have different concerns. How do you ensure that they are socialised with other dogs? Should you have him or her neutered or spayed? Is microchipping safe? And of course, what happens if they wander off when out for a walk?

Socialising your dog

Letting your puppy have more freedom may seem like a scary prospect, for example, they could run over to another dog and get bitten or become aggressive. This is exactly why your dog should be socialised from an early age. Both you and your dog need to be able to interpret the body language of other dogs so you can tell when to remove your dog from a situation or when they're just making friends or being playful together. You need to know about the doggy greeting ritual!

The greeting ritual

- When dogs meet for the first time they will sniff each other, this is their way of saying 'hello'. And yes, that does mean sniffing each other's bottoms – some owners interpret this as something sexual or aggressive and pull their dogs away, but this is nothing to worry about. Sometimes one of the dogs may take an instant dislike to the other one after they sniff each other – their body will tense up and they may lunge toward the other dog, they may also bark aggressively and growl. Try not to confuse an aggressive bark (the dog's hackles are up and the ears are pinned back) with a playful bark (the dog may lie down or run round in circles).

- At this point the dogs may show an interest in each other, or they may just move on with whatever they were doing beforehand. If your dog is interested they may lick the other dog's face, wag their tail, playfully jump on the other dog or bark playfully. Humans can also take part in this ritual, by bending down and slowly extending a hand so the other dog can sniff it. If the dog is fine with that then you can stroke it. If the dog appears scared or moves back, don't try and pat him.

Socialising your dog

There are rules it's best to follow in order to socialise your puppy successfully:

- If you meet a new dog that you don't know, put your dog on the lead. If the other owner says 'it's okay' meaning their dog's temperament is fine, let your pooch go over for a little sniff. Never let your dog run over to another pooch, especially when the other dog's on the lead – you don't know if that dog has behavioural issues.

- Just because the other dog barks at your dog or growls, doesn't mean it's about to attack. You should be able to tell the difference between a dog who's just saying, 'come on and play', or 'stay away from me'.

- If the other dog's whole body stiffens up and they stand completely still, take your dog away. Do likewise if the dog crouches down with their head lowered, hackles up and back hair standing on end. This is the sign of fear or aggression and both can cause a dog to attack.

- Remember that friendship with other dogs can't be forced. There are some dogs who just don't get on, in the same way that humans don't.

- If you are handing out biscuits, get both dogs to sit and give them one each.

'Dog owners need to be able to tell the difference between play and aggression.'

> **Tip**
>
> Having a fellow dog owner as a walking buddy can help socialise your dog. He will watch how the other dog behaves and learn how to interact.

Having your dog neutered or spayed

When your dog is older you need to think about whether you want to have them neutered or spayed. For some dog owners this is a very contentious issue – there are some people who firmly believe that nature shouldn't be interfered with. Or others who would like their dog to have puppies so they decide against having the medical procedure. By far, the most popular view is that it's healthier for dogs to be neutered or spayed.

Pros

- In the case of male dogs, having them neutered can prevent hernias, prostrate trouble, aggression towards other male dogs and people. A three-year-old male dog, who hasn't been neutered, is considered by some experts as a prime time for them become aggressive and attack. Having a male dog neutered will also stop them from leg humping – although neutering doesn't have a 100% success rate with that.

- Being neutered will stop male dogs from following female dogs who are on heat; something they have an overwhelming urge to do. Some dogs have even been known to dig their way out of gardens just to get to a female dog on heat.

- Having a female dog spayed will mean that they won't experience being on heat at all. This is good for the dog as they won't be confined to short walks or the garden in case they fall pregnant.

- Female dogs typically have two cycles every year – usually every six to 12 months. During this time they can become restless and untypically aggressive due to the hormonal fluctuations. Their cycles can last for up three or four weeks.

- Female dogs who haven't been spayed, may get an infection in their womb or develop a phantom pregnancy, which can be very dangerous. Spaying also reduces their chances of getting certain cancers, urinary problems and of having ovarian disease.

- It's widely agreed by experts that being neutered or spayed is healthier for your dog.

Cons

- Neutered or spayed dogs can have a tendency to put on weight. This can be controlled by plenty of exercise and a healthy diet. Generally, vets will recommend that you cut down the amount of food you give your pooch by a fifth.

- Neutered or spayed dogs won't be able to breed.

- In both cases the operation is irreversible, so you can't change your mind.

- The operation is not cheap, but then again your dog having puppies, or your neighbour suing you because your dog got their dog pregnant isn't cheap either!

- Some owners worry about their dog going under anaesthetic to have the operation, but the benefits far outweigh the risks. Modern day anaesthetics are very safe, but if you are worried please see 'is it safe?' opposite.

'Many animal charities recommend neutering to reduce the number of abandoned pets.'

Fact

Every year in Britain there are thousands of dogs handed in to charities like the RSPCA and Dogs Trust, either because their owners don't want them any more or simply can no longer care for them. This problem is made worse by there being too many unwanted puppies in this country. That's why every so often vets and local authorities will offer free or discounted neutering for dogs.

How soon can my dog have the operation?

Vets generally recommend that male dogs should be neutered when they are between the age of 6-12 months. Female dogs should have the operation before they go on heat for the first time (around four to six months of age), although some vets do recommend that it be done after they've been in season once. The procedure can be done later but it's not recommended because spaying an older dog, or one that has had puppies, can involve a longer procedure and there can be problems. For instance, there is more chance of female dogs becoming incontinent if they have the operation later. Another reason is the risk of a reaction to the anaesthetic can increase with age.

Need2Know

What happens?

- In male dogs the testicles are removed. In female dogs the reproductive organs are removed.

- The operation is done under sedation and anaesthetic and your dog will have to fast overnight. So no treats on the way to the vet no matter how tempting that can be!

- Before the operation your dog will have a check-up to make sure there are no underlying health issues and during the operation their vital signs will be observed. You may also have to leave your dog with the vet overnight and pick them up in the morning.

- After the operation your pet will be in no pain, but they may have some discomfort for weeks afterwards, it's important to get them to relax and to not lick the wound. If your dog is in any pain contact your vet immediately.

Other things to watch out for are:

- Your dog being lethargic after a few days.

- The incision opening, or a discharge coming out of it, or it turning dark red or purple.

- Some swelling is considered normal. Too much and you should contact your vet.

Is it safe?

The procedure is very safe, although with any surgery or anaesthesia there is a small risk that something may go wrong. But vets carry out these operations every day and are very experienced at doing them.

How soon can I breed my dog?

The first question you should ask yourself is can you guarantee all of the puppies a good home? If the answer is no, then perhaps it's best not to breed your dog.

You should also ask yourself whether you're prepared to get up for early morning feeds and to clean up dog mess. Having a litter of puppies running around may sound like fun, but there's a lot of work involved and the financial outlay is high. Dog breeding will not make you rich.

Is microchipping safe?

Dog charities certainly believe that microchipping is safe and recommend that owners get their pets microchipped. Some politicians agree and there were plans to make all owners in Britain have their dogs microchipped. This is for three main reasons:

- To stop the trade in stolen dogs.
- To prevent dogs being used for antisocial behaviour and violence.
- To cut down on the number of strays by ensuring every dog can be returned to their owner. Dogs Trust, who boast of never putting a healthy dog down, say that a third of stray dogs were reunited with their owners thanks to microchipping.

It's painless and will cost around £10. If your details change they can be updated. The RSPCA often hold free microchipping events, so look out for these on their website or in your local area.

Common behavioural problems

Now your dog is an adolescent you might think your training days are over, however, sometimes problems can occur. Here are some of the most common problems and how to remedy them.

Biting and snapping

Of all the things your dog does, this is the worst, that's why you need to put a stop to it straightaway. This applies equally to small dogs and large ones – being bitten by any dog, no matter its size, is no laughing matter.

- If you're playing when your dog bites you, automatically stop. The message you'll give is that biting puts an end to the fun.

- If they snap when you give them a treat, firmly say 'no,' and don't give the treat. No treats for dogs who bite.

- Growl if your dog bites you. This is how another dog would react. Alternatively let out a high-pitched squeak – dogs hate that sound.

- Never abruptly wake up a sleeping dog, because he's descended from wild animals his reflex action is to bite.

- Sometimes young dogs can bite out of boredom, so make sure your dog has chew toys to bite instead.

Dog mounting

This is when your dog jumps on another dog's back and it appears that he or she trying to get intimate with them – female dogs do this as well. The surprising thing is this is a dominance thing and has little to do with procreation. Usually the dog doing the mounting is insecure. This problem will resolve over time, but if it gets to the stage where your dog is provoking fights then it may be time to talk to a dog trainer.

Jumping up

If your dog jumps on you, turn your back and ignore them. Don't say a word or even act like they're there. Dogs see being given any attention as good. If he does it with other people, ask them not to pet him – that way your dog equates jumping up as something that gets them no attention whatsoever and should stop doing it.

Pulling on the lead

Pulling on the lead is probably the most common reason why owners take their pets to doggy training school. To fix this problem, you should choose which side of you your dog will walk on and stick to it. Then hold the lead in the opposite hand and show him a treat you have in the hand nearest to him.

Slowly start walking, your dog will follow your hand and when they do this say 'heel' and then give a small bit of the treat. Keep going, each time giving more of the treat, saying 'heel' as your dog follows you.

Barking when you're out

Dogs are pack animals. You and your family are their pack, but there is no way you can be there 24-hours a day. If your dog barks when they're alone it's a sign of boredom, anxiety or loneliness – these are all symptoms of separation anxiety. To solve this problem you need to get your dog used to being alone. Here are some tips:

- Don't make a big deal of leaving the home or coming back.

- Leave the TV or radio on, dogs like the sound because they find it comforting.

- In the home don't be too attentive to your dog – ignore them at times so they begin to realise that just because you're there doesn't mean you'll always make a fuss of them.

- Leave your dog alone with a toy or chew.

- Try to take your dog on a walk before you go away. Dogs will get anxious if they need the toilet and they can't go out.

- Leave an old jumper of yours in your dog's bed – the scent will be reassuring.

Not coming when told

Many an exasperated dog owner is to be found standing in a park with an empty lead in their hand because their dog wouldn't come back. One day your puppy may pad alongside you nicely and come when called, the next they may start to ignore your command. You now have the doggy equivalent of a stroppy teenager. To get your dog to come back to you, follow the training advice given in chapter 1 – this should retrain your dog to follow your commands.

Getting help

For more serious behavioural problems, please ask your vet for advice or consult a canine behaviourist or dog trainer. The Association of Pet Dog Trainers was set up in 1995 and all members are vetted. You can find out about trainers in your area by going to www.apdt.co.uk and clicking on 'local dog trainers'.

Books

There's a raft of books out there advising on doggy training issues. One of the best is *The Dog Whisperer: The Compassionate, Nonviolent Approach to Dog Training* by Paul Owens and Norma Eckroate (see book list).

Summing Up

Your puppy is now starting to become an adult and you have to make two of the most important decisions you'll ever make:

- Whether to have your dog neutered or spayed.
- Whether to have your pet microchipped.

Whatever you decide to do, make sure it's an informed decision.

Chapter Three

Feeding and Exercise

Dogs live for two things – dinner time and walkies. But sometimes things can go wrong. These days there are so many different types of dog foods and it can be confusing to know which one is best. So, this chapter will offer tips on what to feed your beloved pet. And, if things go wrong there's also advice on how to help your dog's waistline.

Feeding regime

Knowing how much and how often to feed your furry friend can be confusing. How many calories does your dog need and what type of food is best? There is such a variety of dog food these days, but which one do you feed your dog?

The choice is between dry and wet food, and what is known as the bones and raw food diet (BARF diet). You can, if you wish, combine a dry food mixer with wet food. Many pet owners swear by this. A mixer is not a complete dog food and shouldn't be given on its own.

Dry food

Dry food is a complete food that has been cooked or baked and then diced into small cubes or other shapes. It's considered better for a dog's dental health as it has to be chewed. There are many different varieties and you can get ones tailored to puppies or senior dogs.

Wet food

This is usually in a tin or a foil tray. It's also been cooked and like the dry food it's a complete food that's tailored to your dog's diet. You do need to watch out for additives like food colourings, preservatives and flavourings. They've been linked to health problems in dogs.

The BARF diet

The BARF diet is increasing in popularity. Owners who feed their dog on this regime believe it's the closest their dog can get to their natural diet. As yet not enough research has been done into the health benefits. There are three main concerns about this diet:

- The amount of drugs cattle are pumped full of may make this diet dangerous to dogs, as it may be passed into the meat.

- The meat is raw and uncooked, which means that the bacteria that's usually killed through cooking is still present.

- This diet may make dogs aggressive like they would be in the wild.

'If you can, avoid dog foods that contain colorants.'

> ## Tip
>
> Dogs can have food allergies. Signs can include lethargy and changes in your dog's coat like dry skin, however, check for fleas first as that may be the cause. If your pet does have an allergy there are foods aimed at dogs like him.

How much food

Generally it's best to follow the guidelines on whatever food you buy. How much a dog eats should be based on three things:

- Age.

- Weight.

- Activity level.

Dry foods often contain a measuring scoop so you can ensure you're using the right amount. Tins or trays will tell you how much of the container is appropriate for your dog.

> **Tip**
>
> If your dog has been given a substantial treat during the day, cut down the amount of food accordingly.

How often to feed your dog

Dogs should be fed once or twice a day. If it's twice a day, then they should get one meal in the morning and another in the early evening. Don't feed your dog immediately before or after exercise, as this can cause a twisting of the gut in some dogs. Try not to feed your dog scraps from the dinner table, mainly because of the dangers that human food present for dogs, but also to ensure your dog maintains a healthy weight.

Always have a dish of fresh water available and create an eating area where your dog won't be disturbed during dinner time. Some dogs can become aggressive if someone gets in the way of their dinner.

Overweight pets

It may seem cruel when your pet seems hungry not to feed them, but it wouldn't be kind if they became overweight. Being overweight is bad for dogs because:

- Your dog won't be able to run around and play like other dogs. That is really sad when you consider going out is one of the most important aspects of a dog's life.

- Too much weight places extra strain on the heart and can lead to fatty tissue growing around the heart. An extremely overweight dog's heart can just give up.

- Just like humans, overweight dogs risk diabetes and heart disease.

'I gave Stan a rawhide shoe and he went into a fit. The vet said he was allergic to rawhide.'

Eric, talking about his German Shepherd.

- Overweight dogs end up with joint problems, including early arthritis.

- They can also have respiratory problems, causing them to pant all the time just to get a breath.

- It means you are not a responsible dog owner – just like with children you have to learn to say 'no'. A dog will eat until they make themselves sick if left to their own devices – this is an instinct left over from being a wild animal when they wouldn't know where the next meal is coming from.

Preventing weight gain

- Stop handing out too many treats.

- Don't give your dog scraps from the table. Dogs shouldn't really be given human food because our food is high in salt and sugar whilst a dog's natural diet is not.

- Dogs need exercise, with breeds like collies, spaniels, German shepherds and Labradors needing more than most. They should get this exercise regularly. The mistakes many dog owners make is thinking their dogs need less exercise just because it's cold outside.

- Dogs need ways to exercise that are fun. My dog Benjy loves nothing more than to go for a swim, other dogs love to chase a ball or another toy. Find out what your dog likes and make sure they get plenty of exercise.

- Socialising with other dogs is important. Not only does it fulfil their natural need to be with their own kind, it also gives them exercise.

Tip

If you genuinely don't think you are overfeeding your dog and yet they have piled on the pounds, have a vet examine him. There may be an underlying health problem such as an underactive thyroid. In dogs this is called hypothyroidism and it is treatable.

Is your dog overweight?

It can be hard for someone to realise that their dog is overweight. Usually, as dog lovers, we see our pets through rose-tinted spectacles. That's why it's important to listen to others, especially when in most cases the weight gain is so gradual we may not have noticed it at all.

Has your vet told you your dog is overweight? If anyone will know if a dog is overweight it's a vet, they see dogs of all shapes, sizes and breeds and know when a dog is just a bit on the podgy side or obese.

Other ways to tell if your dog is overweight include:

- See if your dog's collar has suddenly got tighter. Remember though, this doesn't apply to puppies because they are still growing.

- See if you can feel your dog's ribs. If it's hard to feel them because they are under a layer of fat, then the chances are your dog is overweight.

- See if your dog has a visible dip in his tummy, or if it hangs down like a human beer belly. A doggy beer belly – without the beer of course – is not good news.

- See if your dog's breathing has become laboured. This indicates unhealthiness and extra strain on the heart and lungs.

- Another indicator of overweight or unhealthiness is if your dog doesn't want to go out.

Help, my dog is overweight!

Try not to panic, this is a common problem that can be solved. Whatever you do, stay away from crash diets, these are not healthy for your dog.

- Try a low-fat, easy-to-digest dog food – this could be a food that has lamb, chicken or fish in it.

- Ask your vet for advice. They may be able to suggest a diet plan or a food you can try that has worked for their other patients.

- Cut back on treats.

- If you need to give your dog treats, make sure to use ones that will encourage exercise, e.g. rawhide chews if he's the kind of dog who'll throw it up in the air and get you to chase him.

- Ultimately, losing weight is all about your dog using up more calories than they take in. Basically that means more exercise.

- Have a look at www.petsgetslim.co.uk for tips. You'll discover that you are not alone and there are lots of ways to help your dog lose weight.

Dog with no appetite

There may be an underlying health reason why your dog won't eat. Take them to the vet for a check-up, the vet may weigh your dog to see if they're underweight.

A dog with no appetite can be a sign of something serious, especially if they're reluctant to go out too. However, it may be solved by something as simple as changing their dog food – some dogs can be picky eaters.

Exercising your dog

Now we've dealt with food, it's time to look at your dog's other favourite thing – walkies. That means finding the right lead or harness for you and your dog.

Types of leads and harnesses

- Traditional lead – probably best for a smaller dog or for dogs who walk well on the lead and don't pull.

- Halti – this controls a dog from the chest and shoulders rather than the neck, and is considered a kinder way to deal with a dog that has a tendency to pull as it doesn't choke them. There's also a version of the Halti to go on your dog's head – the downside of this version is that some people assume it's a muzzle because your dog bites.

- A harness – if your dog is on the big side, like a Great Dane, a German shepherd or a boxer, this may be the answer to your prayers. A dog can be easily controlled with one of these without being choked. The one downside is there are some dogs who, no matter how hard you try will simply not wear them.

How much exercise should a dog get?

Dogs who don't get enough exercise can become overweight and even depressed. But how much is enough?

A general rule of thumb is that as well as toilet walks, most dogs need around two walks a day of about 30 minute's duration. But this will not be the case if you own a Chihuahua or a dachshund! If you have a more active dog, like a springer spaniel or collie they may need much more.

Don't make the mistake of thinking that all small dogs only need toilet walks. Some small breeds, like Jack Russells and fox terriers, can't get enough exercise.

If you want to know whether your dog is getting adequate exercise, watch what they do in your home. Do they exhibit any destructive behaviour? This may include chewing things, howling, digging up the carpets and even urinating. If any destructive behaviours like this are happening, your dog may just be telling you they need more walkies!

Mental activity

As well as physical exercise, your dog also needs to be mentally stimulated, you could try:

- Taking a Frisbee, ball or other toys on walks to throw.
- Buying him challenging toys. You can put small, low-fat treats inside these and your dog has to use their canine wiles to get them out or not!
- Playing hide-and-seek – only do this when there is someone with you to keep an eye on your dog as you don't want them running off and urinating on someone's bike!
- Playing tug games. There are special toys for this or you could make your own.

'I realised I wasn't giving Arnie enough exercise when I came home to find he'd made a meal of the sofa.'

Sally Anne.

Summing Up

- The two most important things in any dog's life are feeding and exercise. If you get these two things right, you will have a happy and healthy dog.

- There are many different dog foods on the market – the important thing is to feed your dog something they like and that is healthy. Remember, dogs shouldn't really be given human food at all.

- If your dog is overweight you are putting them at risk of bad health, there are many ways to help your dog lose weight – it's really important for you to help your dog maintain a healthy weight.

- Exercise is really important for your dog, this will keep them physically healthy and if you can combine it with something mentally challenging this will really benefit your dog. Look out for destructive behaviour or weight gain, this may indicate they are not getting enough exercise.

Chapter Four

Doggy First Aid

It's a sad fact of life that at some point your dog may be injured or get sick. It might be a cut paw or a strained ligament, but you may need to know how to deal with it before you go to the vet. The advice given in this chapter is for guidance only – make sure you contact your vet for professional advice.

A doggy first aid kit

Most of us think nothing of having a first aid kit at home for our families, even if it's just some plasters and painkillers in a medicine cabinet. So, why should your pet be any different?

What should a doggy first aid kit contain?

- A pair of tweezers for pulling out thorns, splinters, stings and ticks that lurk in Britain's countryside. You can also buy tick removal tools from pet shops.

- Cotton balls or anti-bacterial wet wipes for cleaning wounds and sterile gauze pads to clean and cushion wounds.

- A pill crusher. We all know how hard it is to get a dog to take his medicine, with this device you can break pills up for adding to your dog's food.

- A dog boot or shoe. These are not to be confused with the type of canine shoes that celebrities like Paris Hilton put on their pampered pooches! These shoes are made of special hard-wearing materials that stop an injured paw from getting wet and keep it warm. You can buy Mikki dog boots which are ideal for paw pad injuries and stop infection. They are made of vinyl and non-slip PVC soles. By far the sturdiest type of boots I have found are made out of a material called neoprene. They are so good because they bend with the dog's paw without causing them any discomfort at all. Available in pet stores.

- A blanket to keep your dog warm.

- A flea comb. Sadly, fleas are a fact of life for dog owners – see chapter 6 for details of how to deal with fleas.

- Bandages and surgical tape.

- Hydrogen peroxide. This should be the 3% solution. It has dual uses. Firstly it can induce vomiting if your dog has eaten something bad and the vet tells you to make your dog sick. It also sterilises wounds.

- A syringe. You may have to add medication in liquid form to your pooch's food on the advice of your vet.

- An antihistamine like Piriton or Benadryl. This is useful if your dog has an allergic reaction to, say, a bee sting. Ask your vet what the correct dosage is for your dog.

- It may also be useful to have some kind of painkiller/anti-inflammatory suitable for dogs, like Rimadyl, in your kit – keep it out of the reach of young children. You will need to ask your vet for this. Never give your pet one without asking your vet first as it's vital you get the correct dose.

- It may be helpful to have a diagram of how to do CPR and the Heimlich manoeuvre in your first aid kit – when an emergency arises you might need it to remind you what to do

---

Tip

Make sure you write down the name and number of your vet, including the emergency out-of-hours number, in your first aid kit. You may need it close at hand in an emergency. Also, ensure your dog's vaccination records are available in case of emergencies.

Doggy first aid

In some circumstances it will not be possible to speak to your vet before administering first aid to your dog. For example, I was on a walk with my dog, Benjy, when he got a stick stuck in his throat. It was lodged horizontally across his throat and I needed to act very fast to help him. I put my hand in his mouth to pull it free – I was very lucky that he didn't struggle or bite me when I did this. But if I hadn't intervened so quickly he could have died. It's because of emergencies – most of which won't be life-threatening – like that it's essential you know some basic first aid.

How to treat a cut paw

■ Inspect the paw for any dirt, glass, grass, nails or objects of any kind. Also check that there's nothing embedded in the cut. If there is, this is when your first aid kit comes in handy – try to remove the object with the tweezers.

■ If one of your dog's claws is broken you will need to trim it to prevent it getting caught on things and irritating the wound. If the claw is broken off at the base your dog needs veterinary treatment.

■ Clean the paw. The best way to do this is with lukewarm water or an antiseptic wet wipe.

■ If you have some, put special dog antiseptic cream on the wound. Your vet will be able to advise you. Don't use human antiseptic treatments as this can be too strong for animals.

■ If the cut is a big one, apply a bandage. To keep the bandage dry you can buy special dog boots or use a torn plastic bag. A sock can protect the wound but won't keep it dry.

■ Regularly check the wound. If it looks infected (there's swelling, it's red and irritated-looking or there's a discharge) take your dog to a vet immediately.

■ If the cut won't stop bleeding apply some sterile gauze pads as a pressure bandage. After 10 to 15 minutes the bleeding should stop.

■ If it's a small cut, don't bandage it as it will heal better with fresh air on it. But don't forget to clean the paw after each trip outside.

- If you're in any doubt, your dog seems to be in distress or you feel it's necessary please take your dog to the vet after administering these basic first aid methods. The most important thing is the health of your dog.

Broken bones

If you suspect your dog has a broken bone you should contact the vet without any delay.

If your dog swallows something bad

If your dog eats or swallows something they shouldn't have, take them to the vet. The vet can do an X-ray to see what has been swallowed. If it's something that can be passed when your dog goes to the toilet, they will let nature take its course. If it's something dangerous that may puncture your dog's stomach they will have to do an operation to remove it. If this is the case, don't worry as vets do these types of operations all the time.

'If you suspect your dog has a broken bone contact the vet immediately.'

If your dog gets run over

If your dog gets run over you may feel an overwhelming urge to pick them up, but that may do more harm than good. If your dog is very light then it is okay to pick them up gently, but if your dog is heavier, you should only move them onto a flat surface with someone else's help. Hugging an injured dog is not a good idea as you may hurt them even more. Obviously though, you shouldn't leave them on the road.

Your dog may have internal bleeding or other injuries like broken bones, so it's best to place the dog on a flat surface like a plywood board, or if you don't have anything like that wrap them in a blanket. Get someone to help you.

- Keep your pet as steady as you can when you lift them or you may exacerbate their pain.

- Take your dog to the vet as soon as possible. Ideally, one person should drive whilst the other sits in the back of the car stroking and reassuring the dog.

- If the dog is in too much pain to be moved, then phone the vet. They may be able to come out and see your pet and administer a pain-killing injection or sedative at the scene.

If your dog gets attacked by another dog

If your dog gets attacked by another dog you should check for any injuries. Is your dog bleeding, yelping, or holding their paw awkwardly? If so, you should get immediate advice from your vet.

If your dog needs veterinary treatment, the owner of the attacking dog may be liable. It may also be worth contacting the police as it is an offence under the Dangerous Dogs Act (1991) to allow your dog to be dangerously out of control in a public place. However, this only applies if the other dog wasn't wearing a collar or wasn't on a lead and your dog was. It's rare that the police act, but if they do visit the other dog's owner, it might make that person think more seriously about preventing it from happening again.

Firework phobia

Each year, especially around 5th November, lots of fireworks go off and this can cause some distress for dogs. Here are a few tips to help your dog cope with all the noise:

- It's important to keep your dog in your home environment when fireworks are going off.

- Turn the TV on or put on some music, as this will help to drown out the sound of fireworks.

- Restrict walks to daylight hours and only take your dog for quick toilet breaks.

- Someone should stay in with your dog when the worst of the noise is going on.

- If your dog is a bundle of nerves and nothing can calm them down, then there are sedative type medications your vet can suggest. One of the best is Dorwest Herbs Scullcap and Valerian tablets. They have no side effects and are available from vets and pet shops.

'Scullcap and Valerian tablets can help calm dogs on fireworks night.'

How to give a dog pills

The easiest way to do this is in some food, but sometimes the direct approach is needed. You have three options:

- Use a pill-giver or giving gun, which has a syringe-like barrel and plunger. There are two claws on the end of the device that place the tablet next to your dog's throat. This should only be used as a last resort and it can help to turn pill-giving into a game.

- Tablet biscuits or canine tablet pockets – these are treats with holes in them where you can place the pill.

- Bribery – put the tablet in a piece of food like cheese or ice cream, only use a very small amount as human food is not really supposed to be eaten by dogs.

Sickness and diarrhoea

The best thing to do in this case is to check there's no blood in the diarrhoea. If there is this may be a sign they have hurt themselves straining to go to the toilet. A little blood once or twice is normal, but if it's worse than that contact your vet right away.

To help your dog recover, the best thing to do is to starve them for 24 hours – only give them water. Their stomach should have settled down by then and then you can think about giving them something to eat. For that, something like rice marinated in a meaty stock cube or with some tuna to make it tasty, is ideal. The rice will bulk up their stomachs, so no more diarrhoea. However, consult your vet if you are in any doubt about the health of your dog.

What if I can't afford a vet?

The PDSA, the charity 'for pets in need of vets' offer free veterinary treatment to those on low incomes. You need to satisfy their criteria:

- Live in the catchment area of a hospital or vet.

- Be in receipt of either housing benefit or council tax benefit.

For details of your nearest PDSA vets or veterinary hospital either go to their website at www.pdsa.org.uk and click on the link for 'find us' or search your local directory for details. There's bound to be one near you as there are currently 47 PetAid hospitals up and down Britain. Although treatment is free you may be asked for a donation.

The Blue Cross also offer veterinary services to those on low incomes or means tested benefits, and have a fleet of animal ambulances to help take the pets of housebound people for treatment. You'll be asked if you will make a donation towards the cost of the treatment and the charity mainly exists to help the elderly and housebound who can't take their pet to a vet. The charity has four hospitals – in Grimsby, Hammersmith, Merton and Victoria. See www.bluecross.org.uk and click on 'veterinary services' for further details.

Dogs Trust may offer financial help or free neutering for your dog. This is only available in certain areas and again you must be on benefits. Occasionally, councils and local authorities run free or discounted vaccination months for pets to encourage pet owners to look after their pet's health.

However, if you are worried about the costs of vet bills and of keeping and looking after a dog, perhaps you should ask yourself whether having a dog is a good idea.

What if I don't qualify for help?

Talk to your vet as soon as you can and ask if they have a payment plan.

Summing Up

- If you know the basics of doggy first aid you will be able to deal with small injuries your dog might have. If you suspect something more serious or broken bones see your vet immediately.

- There is help available for those on low incomes who may find themselves facing large vet bills. Have a look for your local PDSA veterinary surgery.

Chapter Five

Dangerous Foods for Dogs

The family home can be full of things that can cause a dog harm if eaten. In this chapter, as well as naming those things, we'll also look at what to do if your dog somehow gets his paws on items on the doggy banned list.

Chocolate

By far the most harmful thing in our homes is chocolate. In 2008, *The Daily Mail* newspaper reported that vets had seen a 50% increase in the number of patients who had fallen ill after eating chocolate. Despite the fact there have been several high profile campaigns by pet charities like Dogs Trust and the PDSA to warn pet owners of the dangers of human chocolate, there are still people who believe that it's okay to give chocolate to dogs, but it is never safe.

Chocolate intended for human consumption contains theobromine, which, even in small doses, can kill dogs. That's why these days you can buy specially formulated chocolate for dogs from supermarkets and pet stores.

What do I do if my dog eats chocolate?

If your dog does eat any chocolate, don't panic, chocolate poisoning is usually caused by a build-up of the toxin over a long period of time. If it's one bar of normal chocolate your dog has eaten, then the chances are they will be fine, but phone your vet to be on the safe side.

'Chocolate is one of the most common causes of dog poisoning in the UK, but it is one of the most preventable.'

Dogs Trust.

If it's rich chocolate, like Belgian chocolate for example, or your dog has eaten a lot of chocolate, say a whole Easter egg, then take them to the vet immediately. With timely medical intervention your pet's life can be saved.

How can I spot chocolate poisoning?

Dogs with chocolate poisoning will often be sick (the vomit may contain amounts of chocolate) and have diarrhoea. They will be restless and hyperactive and have pain in their stomachs (to check for this put your hand lightly on their tummy). These symptoms will get worse and your dog may start to twitch and tremble and have trouble walking. They also may start to drool and need to drink a lot of water. In extreme cases the dog may go into convulsions.

The symptoms might not begin until hours after your dog has eaten chocolate as it takes dogs longer to digest, so if you find your dog has eaten some chocolate keep an eye out for these symptoms.

How it's treated

Vets will normally give a dog something to make them sick, if they haven't already vomited. If they have been sick, anti-vomiting drugs will be given. Then something is given to absorb the poison in the intestine like activated charcoal. Your dog will be given fluids intravenously to prevent dehydration.

Sadly, chocolate isn't the only foodstuff that dogs shouldn't eat. There are many others.

Bones

It seems like the most natural thing in the world to give a dog a bone, but bones can be dangerous. Small ones (from chicken) can stick in a dog's throat causing them to choke and if the bone is sharp it could even puncture a lung. From a larger bone, bits can break off and become embedded in a dog's throat.

'It tends to be scavenging-type dogs, like Labradors and Jack Russells, that find chocolate and are attracted to the smell.'
Alexander Campbell, Veterinary Poisons Information Service.

If you want to give your dog a bone, which many dog lovers do, especially when they subscribe to the BARF way of feeding their dog (see chapter 3), then an uncooked one is best because it's less likely to splinter.

There are those who believe that sticks can be just as dangerous for dogs, but that's a judgement you will have to make for yourself.

Tip

If you want your dog to have something to chew, there's plenty of rawhide chews and bones to choose from.

What to do if a bone gets stuck

One of my dogs used to steal chicken bones. He was a climber, so no matter how high up they were put, he always managed to steal one. What I had to do when that happened was try to remove the bone from his mouth using two fingers and a thumb to grasp the bone and pull it clear. If the bone was further down, putting fingers in his mouth would cause him to gag and the offending bone would drop out.

However, this is only to be done if you accept that you may end up getting bitten. The advice given here is from personal experience only and if you are in any doubt please contact your vet for advice. They might be able to give you instructions on what to do over the phone.

'Vets have access to a 24-hour helpline Veterinary Poisons Helpline. So no matter what your dog has swallowed they will know how to treat them.'

Tip

Did you know that you can also perform the Heimlich manoeuvre on dogs to expel whatever they are choking on? This is only to be used when it's an emergency and you don't have enough time to get to the vet.

Tea and coffee

The caffeine in tea and coffee can cause similar poisoning to chocolate in dogs. Caffeine can also cause an irregular heartbeat and damage a dog's central nervous system. This applies particularly to smaller dogs as it only takes small amounts to poison them.

Grapes, raisins and sultanas

Most dogs can't digest grapes, raisins and sultanas, eating them can lead to renal failure. In some cases small dogs have died after eating just a few grapes.

Onion

Whether uncooked or cooked, onions should be avoided because they can cause anaemia in dogs as a result of a toxic chemical they contain. Onions can also cause breathing difficulties.

Alcohol

Alcohol can affect a dog's central nervous system and heart, and in extreme cases kill them. Avoid your dog ingesting alcohol at all costs.

Cheese

Dogs like cheese, but that doesn't mean it's good for them in large amounts because cheese contains high levels of fat and salt. Cheese has also been known to affect a dog's pancreas and to give them diarrhoea.

Milk

Just like human beings, dogs can be lactose intolerant. Symptoms are smelly wind and a bloated tummy. If your dog shows any of these signs after having some milk it's best to stop.

Xylitol

This sweetener is found in sugar-free foodstuffs, like chewing gum and biscuits and it's recently been discovered that it's toxic to dogs.

Raw foods

Giving your dog raw egg used to be considered good for their coats, but these days it's best not to give them this as they could end up with salmonella. Also avoid raw meats like liver, without cooking they can contain harmful bacteria like antibiotic-resistant salmonella. Remember, in the wild dogs would eat fresh meat straight from a kill.

'Most human medicines are not safe for dogs, this includes vitamin supplements.'

Tip

It can be difficult to remember what foods you should or shouldn't give your pet. So, why not make it easy and pin a list to the fridge or cupboard door? If you have children, you could get them to help you make a wall chart.

What to do if your dog eats one of these foods

Talk to your vet and explain what has happened. You might not have anything to worry about, but if your dog needs first aid they will tell you what to do.

Other substances that can harm dogs

- Human vitamin supplements – these should never be given to dogs unless instructed by a vet. There are special dog supplements that have the right dosage appropriate to a dog's size and metabolism. Iron supplements are particularly harmful to dogs.

- Human medicines – because of their human-like qualities, we can fool ourselves into believing that dogs are the same as us, but they're not and that's why they shouldn't be given the same medicines as us. Although there are human medicines that are suitable for dogs, the dosage they need will not be the same. For this reason, human medicines should not be given to a dog without first asking a vet. Drugs that don't suit dogs include Paracetemol and Ibuprofen, which can cause permanent kidney and liver damage, and even kill.

- Antifreeze, de-icer and rat poison – they may look like the most unappetising thing ever, but to dogs the sweet taste is irresistible, that's why it's best to always wipe up any spills. Containers should be placed high up where a dog can't reach them and rat poison should never be used anywhere that dogs can access. However, there is an antidote for rat poison if you can get to the vets in time. In the case of antifreeze you need to get treatment for your dog within 12 hours of consumption.

- Weedkiller – dogs may consume this by accident, like when they are eating grass. For that reason it's best not to put any down if you have a pet.

If your dog consumes, or you suspect they have consumed, a harmful substance, follow the steps below:

- Take your dog to the vet right away. Call en route and ask if there is anything you can do to help your pet. You may be asked to try and get your dog to be sick by giving them hydrogen peroxide (available from the chemist). At the surgery they may want to induce vomiting and then administer an antidote for the poison. In the case of rat poison, vitamin K is used.

- Take a sample of the bottle showing what they have eaten.

- Don't wait until symptoms appear to act. Not all poisons are fast acting so if you know your dog has consumed something harmful but they appear to be unaffected, you should still take them to the vet.

Summing Up

It's best to stick to giving dogs their own food and treats and not the human versions. They should definitely not be given:

- Chocolate.
- Small bones.
- Caffeine.
- Grapes.
- Onion.
- Alcohol.
- Large amounts of cheese.
- Sweetener.
- Human vitamin supplements.
- Human medicines.

Things like antifreeze, rat poison and weedkiller should be kept away from dogs at all times.

If you are in any doubt about what's safe for your dog, or you're worried they have eaten something harmful, phone the vet immediately.

Chapter Six

Fleas and Other Nasties

No matter how careful you are, at some point your dog is likely to become infested with these little bloodsuckers. They may come from another dog, a cat (the cat flea is the most common flea on cats and dogs) or even from a wild animal your dog has come into contact with, like a rabbit or a hedgehog.

What are fleas?

Fleas are tiny wingless insects that jump rather than fly. The mouth of these parasites is specially designed for piercing the skin of the host animal, whose blood they drink. In dogs they can cause skin irritation and anaemia (especially in puppies, older dogs and dogs who have been ill recently).

Flea eggs hatch very quickly in the summer. In autumn and winter it may not be until you turn on the central heating that you realise you have a problem when the eggs start hatching.

Has your dog got fleas?

Fleas can be difficult to detect, but there are some telltale signs:

- Your dog may start obsessive scratching or cleaning themselves.

- Your dog may develop a skin infection. Many dogs are allergic to flea bites.

- If you turn your dog over onto their belly and inspect that area and the hind quarters, you may see fleas. They will look like jumping black dots, although in fact they're more of a reddish-brown colour.

- If you can catch one of the suckers – a metal flea comb is best to do this as they are very fast – squish it in a hanky or piece of kitchen towel. If it looks red then it's a flea.

- You are more likely to catch pieces of flea faeces than to see a flea. To find the faeces comb your dog with a flea comb and empty the comb onto white paper or kitchen towel. Flea dirt will look like tiny black flecks and when you wet it, these specks will turn red.

Outwardly there may be no signs at all that your pet has fleas, even vets admit that they have missed fleas.

What do fleas do?

'It's estimated that only about 10% of the flea population is actually on your pet.'

Fleas drink your dog's blood and once they've had their fill, they lay eggs, usually on carpets, bedding or furniture. The undigested food they excrete will end up on your carpet.

Fleas have four stages to their life cycle:

- Egg – the adult flea lays eggs on their host. A female can lay up to 50 a day. These then fall off your pet and onto your carpet, bedding and floorboards.

- Larvae – flea eggs can hatch in as little as two days. Once the larvae emerges, they live off the faeces of the adult fleas and bits of human skin.

- Pupae – the flea larvae make a cocoon where the adult flea develops. Pupae is the last stage before the adult flea develops. Fleas can remain in this stage for up to a year, which is why a flea problem may seem to go away and then come back. Things like humidity and vibrations encourage the flea to emerge from the cocoon.

- Adult – now there are more fleas to lay eggs and start the whole horrible process all over again.

My dog has fleas

If your dog has fleas your home will too, so it's vital you treat your home as well as your dog.

Here are the steps you need to take:

1. Get a good quality flea treatment from your vet.

Frontline is considered the best and the safest treatment as it's not absorbed into the body – it only coats the fur. There are two kinds – Frontline Spot On, you don't need a prescription for this treatment and Frontline Combo, available only on prescription, this medication not only kills fleas, it also has a second ingredient that sterilises them so they can't breed. It's applied using a pipette (a squeezable tube) to the skin at the back of your dog's neck. There are different doses for different weights of dog, including one aimed at puppies. You can get cheaper flea treatment alternatives, including pills, but they're less effective, Frontline kills any fleas that come into contact with it within 24 hours.

Once Frontline is applied, dogs should be kept away from cats as the larger dose given to dogs can harm them. Don't touch the neck of your dog for a while after application in case you get the medication on your hands.

If you have a puppy with fleas, contact your vet for advice on treatment. Puppies under eight weeks old and dogs under 2kg in weight should not be given Frontline. It's unusual but if your pet has a reaction to the flea treatment, contact your vet immediately for advice. Always use the proper doses as given on the instructions.

2. Wash your dog's bed at a high temperature.

You should wash your dog's bed to get rid of any eggs, larvae or adult fleas that may be on it, preferably on a 90-degree wash. Do the same with your bedding and all the soft furnishing in your home, that includes cushion covers, throws and pillows. Also wash all soft toys and curtains.

3. Vacuum your carpets, sofa and chairs at least once a day.

By vacuuming you will pick up fleas, eggs, larvae and even pupae and stop the life cycle that causes fleas. Once you have finished, empty the vacuum bag right away as eggs can still hatch and fleas can survive hovering. Tie the contents tightly into a bin bag so it's airtight, if you can, burn it but if that is not practical put it in another bin bag and tie it tightly.

4. Use a household flea spray on your home.

That includes places your dog hasn't even been as fleas live on humans too and will come off your clothes when you move around. Ensure you follow the instructions on the can. Acclaim is considered one of the most effective you can buy (it also kills ticks and dust mites), but there are many others. Generally though, the cheaper the spray is the less chance it has of being effective.

Before you use the spray, you should get everyone out of the room. Cover any food and drink, including your dog's bowls. After you've given the spray enough time to work, it's wise to leave the windows wide open and air the room for at least 10 minutes before anyone re-enters it.

Alternatively you can buy flea bombs. You set these off in a room once you have cleared it. You must leave the room for two hours and when you come back open all the windows and allow it to air for a while. Wash any residue off your furniture. Unlike sprays, which rely on users spraying them everywhere, flea bombs cover the whole room.

'You must use good quality products to treat your pet and your home, or the flea problem will stay.'

5. Regularly groom your dog.

You should be grooming your dog regularly as fur can get matted – especially if you own certain breeds like poodles or Old English sheepdogs. When your dog has fleas this is not a pleasant task, but it's one that needs to be done in order to get rid of the nasty creatures.

Use a metal flea comb and place your dog on a white sheet (this can be boil-washed afterwards) and carefully comb your dog's fur without digging it into their coat. If the flea problem is bad you will be able to catch some of them (squeeze them between your thumb and middle finger to squash), but it will probably mostly be bits of flea faeces you will catch. Look out for flea bites on your dog and clean them and then apply some animal antiseptic cream. If you want you can also bathe your dog in an anti-flea shampoo. Only do this in cold or lukewarm water as hot water will make the itch worse.

If you can't face grooming your pet, go to a professional dog grooming service. They're used to dealing with fleas.

Treating flea bites on humans

Fleas can target humans too. If you've been bitten you'll have a tiny red bump or a wound that won't stop itching. Bites are usually to exposed body parts like the ankles, the feet and the hands. If this happens to you, clean the wound with some antiseptic and apply some calamine lotion to reduce the itching. If you have an allergic reaction, speak to your GP.

Myths about fleas

It's only natural that when our dog gets fleas we feel embarrassed. The truth is all dogs will get fleas at least once. It's just what happens. We can groom and bathe our dogs every day (actually giving your dog a bath that often isn't good for the natural oil in their coats), but all it takes is one flea to land on them and that's it. Talk to other dog owners and you will discover that their dogs have had fleas too.

Ticks

Ticks pose more of a danger to your furry friend than fleas, because in extreme cases they can pass on infections like Lyme disease and cause paralysis. They also attach themselves to any warm-blooded animal, including humans. Found in long grass or plants in wooded areas, ticks love nothing more than waiting for a passing host and climbing onto their body where, unseen, they will feast on their host.

'When my dog had fleas, I added flaxseed oil to his diet to stop his skin getting inflamed.'

Sophie, dog owner of 30 years.

How to find ticks on a dog

Ticks tend to latch onto parts of your dog where there is little or no hair and they can really sink their mouthparts into the skin. Popular places are within skin folds, in and around the ears and on the back of a dog's legs. I have found ticks on my dog's flanks and even one above his eye. Ticks are opportunists.

The first thing you may notice is a tiny lump on your dog's coat that looks like a mole. Ticks, by that stage, will have little brown legs and bloated pale grey bodies (from all the blood they've sucked). If you notice them before that they will look like a small brownish skin-coloured wart.

The good news is that ticks can be stopped by using certain medications, including Frontline. Frontline will kill ticks within 24 hours and they will fall off, limiting the chance of them harming your dog.

Removing ticks

Ticks are easier to spot than fleas and there are tick removal tools that will make getting them off your dog simple. Alternatively use tweezers.

To remove a tick, take hold of the body and twist anti-clockwise. Ticks burrow in clockwise, so going the opposite way will ensure the head comes off.

Dispose of the tick by squashing it in a paper towel to make sure it's dead or flushing it down the toilet. Clean your dog's wound (ticks often leave a lump) and put some animal antiseptic cream on the area.

Don't try and pick and squeeze at a tick like it's a spot or put whisky on it. This may cause it to regurgitate back into your dog's bloodstream, giving your dog an infection. Don't try a lit match either to burn the tick as some hikers have been known to do.

Worms

Puppies are the most susceptible to worms. According to www.vetbase.co.uk, a site where advice is given by qualified vets, puppies need to be wormed every two weeks from the age of two weeks old until they are 12 weeks old and then every three months. Vets recommend that adult dogs should be wormed every three to four months. Apart from medication, there is no other way to prevent worms.

Tablets are the most popular way of worming a dog. The appropriate number of tablets (based upon your dog's weight and age) should be given with a small amount of food. Medication can also come in liquid form which you add to food as well.

Occasionally, worming tablets can have side effects, i.e. make a dog sick or give them diarrhoea.

Ear mites

These microscopic mites may be living in your dog's ear canal and that's why your poor pooch keeps shaking their head. Ear mites are very difficult to detect and your vet may need to take a scraping from your dog's ear and even then they might not show up. Treatment usually involves a canine ear cleaner and putting in some drops.

If you have other pets they need to get treated too as ear mites can spread.

Summing Up

- Fleas may be every dog lover's nightmare, but you can get rid of them by treating your dog and your home thoroughly to kill any eggs, larvae, pupae or adults left lurking around. This will prevent them reappearing at a later date.

- Ticks must be removed by getting hold of the body and then twisting them anti-clockwise. It's vital to get rid of the whole tick and not leave the head stuck inside your dog's body.

- Dogs need to be regularly wormed. Speak to your vet about your pet to ensure you are worming them regularly enough.

- Ear mites can be a problem, look out for your dog shaking their head and visit the vet for the correct treatment.

Chapter Seven

Travelling With Your Dog

Travelling with your dog has never been easier thanks to the Pet Travel Scheme and animal passports. And these days, if your dog meets certain criteria they might not even need to be placed in quarantine.

If you're thinking of travelling abroad with your dog, you should ask yourself, is it really essential that my dog comes with me? Talk it through with anyone else who is going and think about your dog. Although dogs can adapt quickly to new surroundings, they are creatures of habit.

If you're going away on holiday, perhaps your dog could be cared for by a friend or family member for the time you're away? If you are emigrating it may be better to organise your new life and get settled before your dog arrives. If you can't find anyone suitable or willing to look after your dog while you're away, there are always boarding kennels available.

'If your dog isn't a good traveller, don't take them on holiday.'

Boarding kennels

There are good and bad boarding kennels. If you decide to place your pet in one, there are some things you should do first:

- Go on recommendations of people you trust. Did their dog stay there? Was their dog well cared for during their stay?

- Have a look around first. Do the dogs look happy enough? Are there kennels that are filled with dog mess? This can be a sign that the dogs are not getting enough exercise. Do any of the dogs look distressed? Are the kennels sheltered enough from the elements?

- Speak to whoever will be looking after your dog and ask about the feeding and walking regime.

- If you decide to go ahead, make sure your pet is vaccinated against kennel cough, as in extreme cases this can kill dogs.

- Take along your dog's favourite food (most boarding kennels will not mind if you do this), toys and blanket. This can be placed in the kennel to make your dog feel more at home.

The Pet Travel Scheme

The Pet Travel Scheme (PETS) began in 2004 and was set up so that pets from participating countries, like the UK and the EU, won't have to go through quarantine if they meet the requirements of the scheme. It currently covers dogs, cats and, believe it or not, ferrets. It only covers travel via sea, rail or air at the moment.

'Thanks to the Pet Travel Scheme, more dogs are flying than ever before.'

Initially it was set up so that animals could travel from the UK to EU countries (or in the opposite direction), but other countries have since joined. The other countries include: Japan, Australia, Canada, New Zealand, Singapore, the United States and Bermuda. See www.animalpassports.co.uk for a comprehensive list. On the home page you will see the heading 'countries covered by the Pet Travel Scheme' on the left hand side. Click on 'read more' to get the list.

You can also visit the Department for the Environment, Food and Rural Affairs' (Defra) website for information, go to www.defra.gov.uk. DEFRA regulate the scheme and you can find fact sheets available to download. If you live in Ireland go to www.agriculture.gov.ie.

See the help list at the back of the book for details of the Pet Travel Scheme helpline.

Pet passports

Similar to our human versions, your pet's passport will detail your pet's identity (picture included), have their vaccination history and also contain details of whether they've been treated for ticks and tapeworms.

To qualify for the scheme, stringent conditions must be met:

Need2Know

- Dogs must be microchipped before they travel.

- Rabies vaccinations are compulsory. This includes if your pet has already been vaccinated, no chances are taken where rabies is concerned and after your dog has been vaccinated a blood test must be carried out to ensure they have adequate protection.

- Your dog must have an EU pet passport. Get this from your vet.

- Before your pet leaves the country they must get treatment to prevent ticks and tapeworms. This must happen within a tight time frame, so your vet will advise.

- Arrange for your dog to travel with a recognised transport company on an authorised route – these are listed on the DEFRA website. That way all the animals they come into contact with have received the same treatment and kept to the conditions of travel.

Do dogs need travel insurance?

Travel insurance is a good idea if you don't want to end up lumbered with a big vet bill, or trying to figure out how to get your pet home because you have little or no money. Most 'covered for life' pet insurance plans have travel insurance.

As with all things, read the small print before you sign on the dotted line, all sorts of conditions can apply, for example, you may only be covered when you travel to agreed countries. Get your insurer to explain exactly what that means to avoid misunderstandings and huge bills later.

Travel insurance will include:

- Vet fees – however, there is a limit to what's covered.

- Emergency repatriation – if your dog is ill or injured abroad this will pay to get him home. Usually it will pay up to £500.

- Holiday cancellation fee – if you have to cancel or cut short a holiday because your pet has gone missing, is injured or starts to show signs of an illness, you may get some travel and accommodation costs back.

- Lost paperwork – if you lose the paperwork and you need to get your dog back into the UK, this will cover the cost of getting duplicates and the cost of quarantine.

Checklist for travelling abroad

When you're packing your cases and preparing for the trip, don't forget these:

- Your dog's animal passport – put it somewhere safe and make copies.

- Your dog's collar with your name, address and phone number, it should be worn by your dog at all times.

- Ensure your dog is microchipped. That way if your dog gets lost the chances of you being reunited will be higher. Make sure the chip can be read before you travel – your vet can check this.

- Take any medication your pet needs. It's important that you have a note or copy of the prescription from your vet for this medication.

Frequently asked questions

Q. Can my dog travel on Eurostar?

A. The bad news is that no, your dog can't travel on Eurostar, unless they're a guide or assistance dog. Eurostar doesn't participate in the pet passport scheme, although this may change in the future.

Most ferry companies allow dogs, but only if they remain in a car. Some carriers, like Stenna Line, allow foot passengers to take pets on their Essex to Holland line, as long as they are booked into a kennel in advance. Check before you travel.

Q. Can my dog travel on the Eurotunnel?

A. Yes they can. Eurotunnel's website states: 'Pets are part of the family – so we treat them just as we would any other passenger.'

You must advise the company that you are travelling with your pet when you book. On your return, you'll need to visit the pet control booth so they can carry out the necessary checks. Visit www.eurotunnel.com for further details.

Q. Can dogs travel on normal commuter trains in the UK?

A. Yes they can. Companies don't charge for this. In years gone by, pet owners used to have to pay half fares for their pooches and had to keep them in the guard's van!

Q. Can my dog travel by air?

A. Since the introduction of PETS, flying with your dog has become much easier and there's no worrying about the poor pooch ending up stuck in quarantine for months.

Ask before you book your flight whether the company allow dogs on their planes. Airlines like British Airways, Virgin Atlantic and KLM do, but the majority of low-cost airlines won't let dogs travel. Look at individual websites for details.

Bear in mind that most dogs will have to travel in a crate in the cargo hold and this can be very distressing for some dogs.

Before you fly:

- Make sure your dog is old enough. Most airlines won't let puppies under the age of three months fly.
- Usually you must provide the crate. Make sure it's big enough for your dog to stand up in, turn around in and lie down in a normal manner. If it's not a suitable size airlines will refuse to let your pet travel. Ask for advice if you are unsure.
- Make sure the door of the crate is secure.
- Before you board make sure your dog has had a decent walk and has gone to the toilet.
- It's a good idea not to feed your dog for an hour before travel because they may be sick.
- It may be helpful to ask your vet for some sedatives for your dog to help calm them down.
- Ensure the travel crate is lined with newspaper, because your dog is likely to urinate. Also put in a detachable food and water dish that is also accessible from the outside.

'Most low-cost airlines won't let dogs travel.'

- Put in your dog's favourite blanket or toy, or a piece of clothing that has your scent on it for reassurance.

- Clearly mark the crate on the outside – it's really important to mark which is the right way up.

- Ask the airline what their routine is for caring for the dogs in the hold. Will they feed them and give them water? How often do they check on them? Knowing these answers will stop you worrying.

- It's best that dogs who are pregnant don't fly as the stress of flying can cause problems.

Travelling within the UK

If you want to take your dog on holiday, you may not even need to leave the UK. There are pet-friendly hotels, campsites and B&Bs in this country where you and your dog can have fun without the need for passports and foreign travel.

Pet-friendly holidays

Two of the best websites to find details of dog-friendly accommodation are www.dogfriendlybritain.co.uk and www.petholidays.com.

You may have to pay for your dog to stay in holiday accommodation but with many places it's free.

Summing Up

■ If you're going abroad and you want your pet to come to with you, the first thing you need to do is ask yourself whether it's a good idea. If you decide to take your dog with you make sure you get them a pet passport and follow the guidelines to the letter.

■ If you decide to take him on holiday within the UK, there are dog-friendly establishments up and down the country to choose from.

Chapter Eight

Your Dog and The Law

The Dangerous Dogs Act of 1991 is the most important legislation for dog owners. There are many myths surrounding this law. One of the most common is that it bans people from owning Rottweilers and Staffordshire bull terriers (or Staffies as they are commonly called). This is simply not the case.

Under the 1991 Act, the four dog breeds banned in the UK are:

- 'Pit bull type' dog – some American Staffordshire terriers have been found to be pit bulls, but this is not to be confused with Staffordshire bull terriers who are a different type of dog altogether. Pit bulls aren't a recognised breed in the UK, so a dog is banned if it's considered to be 'of a pit bull type'. This usually means having a very stocky body and long legs.

- The Japanese Tosa.

- The Dogo Argentino.

- The Fila Brasiliero.

These dogs were banned because they are considered to have been bred for fighting or for their aggressive tendencies. It is also an offence to breed from, sell or exchange (even as a gift) a banned type of dog.

There are no defined 'pit bull type' breeds under the Dangerous Dogs Act, this is why the act is seen by some as a contentious issue, it lacks clarity.

If you're worried that your dog is on the banned list ask a vet for advice. For more information on the laws on dangerous dogs, go to www.defra.gov.uk.

The updated act of 1997

Prior to the updating of the Dangerous Dogs Act in 1997, all dogs judged as being one of those breeds if they had certain characteristics that matched, and that includes when they are crossbreeds, were destroyed no matter what their temperament. This led to many dogs being killed when they and their owners had done nothing wrong and animal lovers were appalled. When the Act was amended, dogs deemed to be of a 'pit bull type' were no longer automatically killed and courts could use their own discretion. Well-behaved dogs who qualified were put on the Index of Exempted Dogs.

The owner of a dog on the Index of Exempted Dogs will be given a Certificate of Exemption, which they will need to produce to the police or a dog warden if they are asked to prove their dog is exempt. The dog will need to be neutered, microchipped and tattooed – the owner pays for this. The dog will need to be on a lead at all times in public, be muzzled and the owner must take out insurance against the dog attacking anyone. The pet will also need to be kept somewhere secure where it can't get out.

What can I do if my dog is seized?

If your dog is seized under the Dangerous Dogs Act because it's believed to be a banned breed, one of your first port of calls should be Endangered Dogs Defence and Rescue (see help list). They offer advice about dog-related legal matters and legislation affecting dogs. They campaign for better treatment of dogs who have been seized by police under the Dangerous Dogs Act.

If it is believed your dog is a banned breed you do have some rights under the law.

- Seek legal advice immediately.

- A warrant is needed by police to seize your dog from your home, they cannot do this unless there is a warrant.

- The police will have appointed a breed identification expert who will have made a report stating what breed they consider your pet to be based on its physical appearance. If your dog was seized because it's believed to be a banned breed, it's up to you to prove them wrong. You'll need a dog expert to help you do this.

- It is a good idea to get references for your pet attesting to their good behaviour. The higher the standing in your community that the referees are, the better. This means members of the clergy, doctors, lawyers and councillors are good to ask for a reference.

- If you're found guilty of owning a banned dog, but your dog is not considered to be dangerous and you're a responsible owner, your dog will be returned to you and placed on the Index of Exempted Dogs.

Your responsibilities as a dog owner

For the majority of dog owners, the information about banned breeds doesn't really apply. However, there are some parts of the Dangerous Dogs Act that apply to all dog owners, most notably that it is an offence to allow your dog to be out of control in a public or private place where it is not meant to be.

What is meant by that?

The key words here are 'out of control'. Under the law, that's deemed as being when your dog injures someone (this applies to people only and not other dogs), or your dog behaves in a way that makes someone think they are going to be attacked or bitten.

In some cases it may be considered an offence if your dog attacks someone else's dog, especially if the owner of that dog believes that by intervening to protect their pet they may risk getting attacked by your dog too.

Generally though, the law is only interested when a dog attacks or bites a human being and not another dog. That's not to say though that the owner of the other dog wouldn't have grounds to sue to recoup their vet's bill, but this only applies if their dog was on the lead at the time of the incident.

'The Dangerous Dogs Act is the most important legislation for dog owners.'

The penalty

Under the law you could get up to two years in prison and a fine if you're found guilty of allowing your dog to act dangerously. Your dog could be muzzled or put down. The police and local authorities are the ones who ensure the law is enforced.

Proposed laws

It's a good idea to look out for any new legislation regarding dog ownership to make sure you keep up and have your say. It may soon be compulsory for all dogs to be microchipped and have insurance and there are proposals for a new law that would make you responsible for how your dog behaves in a private place, including your own garden and home. This is mainly to protect postmen, but there are worries by animal charities that dogs may be put down because of their natural instinct to protect their homes and owners from intruders.

'It's an offence to allow a dog to be out of control in public.'

DEFRA.

There are also proposals for New Dog Control Notices (already dubbed 'Dogbos') aimed at misbehaving animals that would force owners to muzzle, leash or even neuter their pets. In extreme cases, dogs could be confiscated or even given to new owners.

The Control of Dogs Act (EIRE)

In the Republic of Ireland there are controls on certain breeds of dogs. They must be muzzled in public at all times and on the lead with someone who is at least 16 years old.

The breeds are – American pit bull terrier, English bull terrier, Staffordshire bull terrier, bull mastiff, Rhodesian ridgeback, doberman, German shepherd, Rottweiler, Japanese Akita, Japanese Tosa and bandogs.

Dog Control Orders

Dog Control Orders came into force in 2006 under the Clean Neighbourhoods and Environment Act and were aimed at tackling not just dog fouling, but also littering. They cover five different areas and breaking the control orders can mean a £75 fixed fine (England and Wales) or £50 for allowing your dog to foul land (Northern Ireland).

- Dog fouling – owners must pick it up and bin it.
- Not keeping a dog on a lead. This doesn't apply to open land or assistance dogs.
- Taking a dog onto land where it's been excluded. During certain months, for instance, dogs are not allowed on public beaches. Where this happens local authorities must put up signs to state this is the case.
- Taking too many dogs onto specified land. This usually means one person taking four dogs or more onto one bit of land.
- Not putting a dog on the lead when asked to by an authorised officer.

These control orders don't apply in Scotland (correct at the time of going to press), but they soon might. If in doubt about which laws apply in your area contact your local authority for details.

Other obligations

Being in control of your dog in public places isn't where your responsibilities end:

- Dogs must have a collar with their name and address – even if they're microchipped. Dogs without collars will be picked up as strays. Local councils are obligated to pick up stray dogs.
- You should always pick up dog foul and bin it.
- You must also pick up dog foul in your garden. It's an offence to allow too much to accumulate, as it will cause a health hazard.

- Dogs shouldn't be allowed in restricted areas designated by your local authority. This may include beaches at certain times of the year and children's play parks.

- In the Republic of Ireland and Northern Ireland you must have a dog license.

- Barking dogs are a nuisance and if neighbours complain you could be served with a notice by the council telling you that unless it stops you may have to get rid of your dog. You may also face eviction from your home if you rent.

- As a dog owner you have a 'duty of care'. This means you must care for your pet and that includes getting them medical treatment if they need it. If you don't you can be prosecuted for animal cruelty and neglect. If you have trouble paying vet fees see chapter 4 for information on options available to you.

Stray dogs

Sometimes dogs escape from homes and it's nobody's fault. If that happens to your dog they could be classified as a stray and picked up by the local dog warden service. If you think this might have happened contact the Dog Warden Service.

What happens to dogs picked up by dog wardens?

- If your dog has a collar or is microchipped they will contact you to let you know.

- Dogs whose owners can't be identified will be taken to council kennels where they will be kept for at least seven days.

- The owner then has seven days to collect their dog. If the owner turns up they will be charged a fixed fee set by the government and a kennelling fee before they are allowed to take their dog home.

- Many councils have registers for lost and found dogs to enable them to reunite them with their owners.

- If the owner doesn't appear, dogs are rehomed or passed on to a relevant rescue charity, like Dogs Trust. Only in very rare cases, if a dog is too ill or is extremely aggressive, is it put down.

Lost or stolen dogs

If your dog is missing it can be a worrying time, there is a strong chance you will be reunited so start searching with the following steps.

- Search for your dog in their favourite places.
- Contact the Dog Warden Service.
- Contact all the vets in your area – a passer-by may have brought in your dog.
- Find out if your local authority has a 'dog line' where you can phone about your missing pet and they'll tell you if they have been found.
- Place 'wanted' posters near where your dog was lost and ask people if they have seen your dog. Ask as many people as you can to look out for similar dogs.
- Contact the police in case they've got your dog – the police have a scanner to check if dogs have been microchipped.
- Place ads in local newspapers and shop windows.
- Register with websites that list dogs that have been lost, found and even stolen. You can post the details of your missing pet on award winning www.dogslost.co.uk. There's also the UK National Pets Register at www. nationalpetsregister.org. Their database is checked daily by vets, police, animal shelters and people all over the UK. Both services are free.

> **Tip**
>
> You can make sure your chances of getting your dog back are high if they've been microchipped and have your name and address on their collar.

Frequently asked questions

Q. If my dog bites someone will he have to be put down?

A. This usually only happens in extreme cases, say if your dog attacks a child.

Q. My dog caused a traffic accident, what are the consequences?

A. You may be liable to pay compensation if your dog causes a traffic accident. This is if it can be proven that your dog caused the accident. This type of eventuality is covered by the third party liability component of your pet insurance. See chapter 9 for details.

Q. What happens if my dog bites an intruder?

A. This depends on the circumstances. If your home is broken into when you are out and your dog bites someone, then no police action will be taken. If you set your dog on an intruder you may be prosecuted and the person they bite may be able to launch a civil suit for compensation.

Q. My dog was attacked by another dog, what are my rights?

A. In this case it's all down to whether the other dog was on the lead and its owner had it under control. If they didn't they are liable to pay your vet costs.

Summing Up

- There are four banned dog breeds under the Dangerous Dogs Act. The 'pit bull type' breed encompasses many different breeds so the law is a little unclear at the moment.

- Not all dogs found to be a banned breed will be put down – well-behaved dogs will go on the Index of Exempted Dogs.

- As a dog owner, it is your duty to have your pet under control in public places under the Dangerous Dogs Act or face prosecution.

- Be a responsible owner by not letting your dog intimidate other people, cleaning up after them, and keeping them on the lead where instructed and where is appropriate.

- Act fast and get the word out if your dog goes missing.

Chapter Nine

Pet Insurance

Once upon a time if you'd asked the majority of pet owners whether they had pet insurance, they'd have looked at you blankly or said no. These days it's become more popular and there have even been calls to make it compulsory for pet owners. This is because too many dogs are ending up in rescue centres because their owners can no longer afford to care for them.

In this chapter we'll try to demystify pet insurance and look at what it will cover and what it won't. However, the advice given here is no substitute for professional advice, policies will vary.

Soon, you may not have a choice about whether to get pet insurance, as there were moves afoot by politicians to make it compulsory for all dog owners to have insurance. This was not for animal health reasons, but so dog owners would have third party insurance in case of their dog attacking someone. These failed, but the plans may be resurrected some day.

'If you decide not to get pet insurance or can't afford it, it's a good idea to put aside some money each month to pay for vet bills.'

Pros of pet insurance

There are many good reasons to get pet insurance. Here are some of the most important:

- If your dog is seriously injured or needs a major operation, pet insurance will cover the cost. That can ease the worry of getting an unexpected vet bill or having your dog put down because you can't afford a vital operation.

- Some pet insurance 'covered for life' plans will often provide cover if your dog causes a traffic accident. The pet insurance would pay for the damage to the driver's car and any personal injuries they claim for. However, plans that cover this are usually the more expensive ones.

- Any ongoing conditions your dog has are covered. This is up to the maximum amount as stated in your policy.

- You can get special puppy insurance which covers dogs from the age of six weeks old.

- Pet insurance firms often have animal charities that they donate money to, so by getting pet insurance you may be helping less fortunate animals.

- Your pet will get 'lifetime cover' as long as you keep paying the premiums. That means any eligible vet bills are paid for the rest of your dog's life.

- Alternative medicine, like herbal medicine and acupuncture, may be included if it's listed in your terms and conditions.

- You may get a discount if you insure more than one dog.

Remember that each individual policy is different. Ask before you sign and remember there is a cooling off period during which you can change your mind and cancel the policy.

Cons of pet insurance

There are downsides to having pet insurance. One of them is the cost, as you could end up giving the insurer more in premiums than they ever pay out.

There are other cons too:

- You will be charged more for certain breeds of pedigree dogs. This is because they need more medical care than the average dog. Those select breeds may include – St Bernard, Pyrenean mountain dog, old English sheepdog, Dogue de Bordeaux, Irish wolfhound, all mastiff breeds including bull mastiff, Rottweiler, Bernese mountain Dog, bulldog, Great Dane and Newfoundland. In the case of Shar-Pei dogs, many insurers will want to see a full veterinary history before they will insure them.

- You may be charged more for older dogs.

- Dogs which are not neutered or spayed, may cost more to insure because they have more health problems.

- Pet insurance will not cover the cost of things like vaccinations and worming. Nor will it cover dog food or bedding, or any day-to-day costs.

- There is also an 'exemption' or 'exclusion' clause in contracts that means pre-existing conditions will not be covered usually from a period of 12 months before you took out the policy. This means any conditions that your dog had symptoms of, you got advice about or your dog was treated for, are not covered. In my case, Benjy had an ear infection when I insured him so anything to do with that or a skin complaint is not covered in my policy. However, this will be stated clearly on your certificate.

- There is an excess charge applied when you claim on your pet insurance. For further details see 'things to ask your insurer' in this chapter.

- Most pet insurers will not pay out for an illness or injury that starts during the first 14 days of cover.

Types of pet insurance

There are three types of pet insurance with key characteristics:

- Annual policy – there's a fixed amount you can claim per condition and you are only covered for 12 months. Any medical treatment needed after that period and you'll need to meet the cost yourself. You can only claim once for the same condition. This type of policy is not for you if your dog has a long-term illness.

- Per condition policy – an illness or condition is no longer covered once the limit is reached and you can't claim for the same condition again. This type of policy is not for you if your dog has an ongoing illness.

- Lifelong cover – If your dog has a long-term illness or condition this is the plan you want. You can claim for the same condition again with the same insurer, but there is a limit to the amount they will pay out each year. This is the most comprehensive form of pet insurance and also the most expensive.

Find the best deal

There are many different insurance providers. Amongst the most well-known are Pet Plan, the PDSA and Direct Line Pet Insurance.

To get the best deal you should shop around. Ask people you know who've got pet insurance for advice and have a look at reviews on the Internet. One of the best sites to do this is www.ciao.co.uk, which has reviews on all kinds of products and services.

Look out for any special deals the pet insurers are offering, such as free insurance for a month or discounts on pet things you might need. There's also often a discount for signing up to one online. Many of the supermarket chains like Tesco, ASDA and Marks & Spencer, also offer pet insurance.

If you want independent advice and quotes then go to consumer comparison sites like Go Compare, Confused.com and Compare the Market. There is also a site that specialises in comparing pet insurance and it has categories like 'fixed amount per condition' and 'unsuitable for long-term illnesses'. Visit it at www.petinsuranceonline.co.uk.

Things to ask your insurer

You will get a printed document with your dog's name on it stating what they're covered for. If you are in any doubt here are the questions you need to ask:

Q. What does my policy cover?

A. With pet insurance it's best not to assume anything. There are 'value' versions that can often be of little or no use to pet owners in the long term. Pet insurance plans can cover more than simple vet bills, they can also cover boarding kennel fees, offer compensation if you have to cancel a holiday because your pet gets ill, and cover the cost of getting your pet back if they're lost or stolen.

There's also 'third party liability' coverage. This means that if anyone is injured, dies or property is damaged because of an accident your pet causes, your pet insurer will pay compensation and costs to the person who sues you and pay your legal costs. However, an excess will apply to most claims you make.

Q. Is it a 'covered for life' policy?

A. If your dog suffers from a long-term illness you should invest in a 'covered for life' policy. It basically means you can claim for the same condition again and again but there is a limit to the amount they will pay out each year. It is the most comprehensive form of insurance but also the most expensive. If you are not sure whether your policy is a 'covered for life' policy you should ask them to confirm either way.

Q. What isn't covered?

A. You should check with your insurer what isn't covered, it's almost as important as what is covered! For example, a clause in the insurance could be that the policy will only pay out during the first 12 months of your dog's sickness, for a condition such as hip dysplasia or arthritis this wouldn't be ideal.

Q. Will the policy only pay out a set amount for certain conditions, regardless of how much treatment actually costs?

A. Definitely check this with your insurer, for example, the treatment might cost £1,000 but the insurer may only pay £800 of that. Never assume that being covered for vet bills means that every penny is covered.

Q. How do I make a claim for vet's fees?

A. Usually you will have to pay the vet and you claim the money back from the insurer using a claim form but some insurers will allow your vet to bill them direct. Check your policy so you know the procedure should you need to make a claim.

Q. Are there any preconditions?

A. Most commonly you'll have to ensure your dog gets a regular dental check and show you take care of your pet's health, check your policy to be sure. Certain breeds are not covered by pet insurance and this includes any dog that is, or is crossed with, a 'pit bull type' dog because this is a dog banned under the Dangerous Dogs Act.

Q. Will I have to pay veterinary excess fees?

'If in doubt about anything regarding your policy don't assume anything, always ask your insurer. Get it in writing if you can, most insurers will be happy to do this.'

A. This is the fee you as the policyholder must pay in the event that you make a claim. This means, unfortunately, that your full vet's fees will never be repaid to you as this is often deducted from the total fee when you are reimbursed, or you may have to pay it up front when you claim. The excess fee may be a percentage or a set fee, ask your pet insurer for the details.

Q. What happens if I miss a premium?

A. Accidents happen, direct debits can go wrong, credit cards are stopped. So, if this happens to you contact the insurer and tell them what's happened. The sooner you get your account back in good standing the better for you and your pet. Check with your insurer that your pet insurance is still valid should you miss a payment, there may be quite strict rules surrounding this so it's better to be safe than sorry.

Summing Up

■ Pet insurance can be a minefield, there are many pros and cons. Make sure you know exactly what your policy covers as well as what it doesn't.

■ Search for a good deal, but make sure it meets your requirements, otherwise it could be rendered useless when you actually need to claim.

■ If you are in any doubt about an aspect of your pet insurance, check the exact meaning with your insurer.

■ If you can't afford pet insurance you should be putting away money each week to pay for vet bills.

Chapter Ten

Special Needs Dogs

For the purpose of this section, special needs dogs are defined as those who need a bit more care than a normal dog because they have health problems. Whether your dog is deaf, blind or epileptic, the good news is that they can still live a long and fulfilling life.

Canine epilepsy

As in humans, canine epilepsy is caused by an abnormality in the brain and the majority of patients are born with it. In most cases the cause is unknown, this is called idiopathic epilepsy. In a small number of cases, a dog sustaining a blow to the head can cause damage to the brain. Male dogs are more susceptible and so too are certain breeds like golden retrievers, German shepherds, Labradors and poodles.

There is no cure for epilepsy, but in the majority of cases medication can help control it, either by reducing the number of fits or stopping them almost completely. Dogs with epilepsy can live long and happy lives.

'Around four in every hundred dogs have epilepsy.'

What to do if your dog has an epileptic fit

■ Make sure that there are no heavy objects around that can fall on your dog's head, or things they can trip on.

■ If your dog's eating something at the time of a fit, take away the foodstuff to avoid them choking.

■ Turn off the TV and any lights. When your dog comes round from the fit, loud noise and bright lights may be frightening.

- Speak soothingly to your dog, try to calm them down and make them feel secure.

- You shouldn't touch your dog when they're having a fit in case you get bitten.

- Phone your vet – if the fit lasts longer than two minutes, doesn't seem to end or your dog keeps going in and out of fits, it can be very serious.

- If your vet has given you rectal diazepam liquid you should use it if the fit lasts two minutes or more.

- Keep a note of when the fits happen, how long they last, their severity and how your dog is afterwards.

How is epilepsy diagnosed?

If your dog has had one isolated fit it does not necessarily mean they're epileptic. A thorough examination will be done and you'll be asked to watch out for any further seizures.

How epilepsy is treated

In many cases, dogs won't need any medication at all. If dogs have cluster fits (more than one fit in the same day) or their fits occur more often than once every four to six weeks, then they will need medication.

The three most common medications are:

- Phenobarbital – this is an anticonvulsant drug in tablet form and should be given with food. One of the side effects can be liver damage, your dog will need a liver function test before starting on the drug and then regularly while they're taking it. The sedative effect can also be quite severe in some dogs, making them dopey and unresponsive and also causing hind leg weakness.

- Potassium bromide – this isn't as popular as phenobarbital because it can take months to work. It has less side effects but it can give the canine patient a sore stomach, so it's advisable to give it twice a day with food.

- Diazepam (also called valium) – this can be given in tablet or liquid form, but is for short-term use only as over time it loses its effectiveness. In liquid form it is commonly used when a dog will not come out of a fit for more than a few minutes or goes immediately into another fit with little or no recovery time. This is called 'status epilepticus' and is highly dangerous and often fatal. Summon the vet immediately if this happens to your dog.

If your dog has epilepsy it's vital you get the rectal tubes of diazepam from your vet. This could save your pet's life.

Tip

Many vets also recommend Scullcap and Valerian tablets from Dorwest Herbs. Visit www.dorwest.com for details.

Other things that can help an epileptic dog include:

- A magnetic collar.

- Avoiding dog food with artificial colourings and additives.

- A synthetic, vegetarian melatonin supplement can also help to reduce the number of fits a dog will have.

- The food supplement epitaur aids the central nervous system in dogs. The central nervous system is where taurine is found, dogs with epilepsy have low levels of this naturally occurring amino acid.

Always talk to your vet before you put your dog on any supplements.

'Dogs with epilepsy can live a long and happy life.'

Arthritis

Most dogs will get arthritis at some stage in their lives, usually from the age of eight onwards, but this can be much younger for some pedigree dogs with a predilection for arthritis, like Great Danes. The good news is there are a host of pharmacy medicines and natural remedies you can use to keep your dog mobile. Speak to your vet about the options.

Arthritis medication can have side effects, so it may be a case of seeing which one suits your dog best. Do your research – speak to other dog owners and go online to doggy message boards to find out what drugs other pet owners have been prescribed and how they're working out.

Does my dog have arthritis?

The symptoms of arthritis are easily misread as signs of old age, you should consult your vet if you notice any of the following symptoms becoming pronounced:

- Your dog is having trouble getting up after they've been lying down for a while.
- You can hear creaking in your dog's bones when they move.
- Your dog develops a noticeable limp that won't go away.

Helping an arthritic dog

The best way to help your arthritic dog is to keep their weight at a normal level and get your vet to prescribe some medication that can help. If your dog has trouble getting into the car or down the stairs, using a ramp could help.

Encouraging your dog to go for a swim on a warm day can also help. If you live too far away from a safe stretch of water, some vet practices offer hydrotherapy.

Blindness

As long as your dog still eats and wants to go out, going blind or losing some of their sight doesn't mean you have to put them to sleep. A good resource for learning how to live with a blind dog is Caroline D Levin's *Living with Blind Dogs* (see book list).

Cancer

Like humans, with treatment dogs can survive cancer – dogs, especially older ones, are susceptible to tumours and sometimes surgery is required. Dogs can also get radiotherapy and drugs therapy, which is a form of chemotherapy. For dogs the dose of any drug is calculated carefully to avoid nasty side effects.

Visit the Animal Cancer Trust at www.animalcancertrust.org.uk for advice (further details in help list).

How you can help

The best way to help a dog with cancer is to ensure your dog keeps eating. If your dog goes off their food, change to something else that they will eat. Consult with your vet if you are unsure what will be safe in conjunction with the cancer treatment.

Deafness

Believe it or not you can teach dogs sign language! There's a book aimed at caring for a deaf dog, written by someone who trains deaf dogs, *Hear, Hear! A Guide to Training a Deaf Dog* by Barry Eaton, is considered the best (see book list).

There's an excellent site set up by people who care for a deaf Dalmatian called Humphrey which has an illustrated guide to hand signs, go to www.deafdal.co.uk.

Diabetes

Dogs can get diabetes too, the signs are similar to those in humans:

- Increased thirst and urination.
- Eating normally, but still losing weight.
- Suddenly developing cataracts in the eyes.

Treatment

Like human diabetes, the canine version can be easily controlled through a mixture of diet and medication. This may involve giving your dog insulin injections to make sure they have enough insulin in their body, your vet will show you how to do this and tell you when to give your dog an injection. You will usually have to give them insulin twice a day. Diabetic dogs who are not treated can develop cataracts and in severe cases die. There are special dog foods for diabetic dogs, ask your vet for advice.

Hip dysplasia

This is a genetic disease that affects the hip joints of dogs, particularly common in some breeds like German shepherds, boxers and Labradors. Some experts blame the booming puppy farm trade for this and too much in-breeding.

The condition is usually diagnosed by X-ray but sometimes that isn't needed. Some dogs with this condition will have mobility problems, but on the whole, with treatment, dogs with hip dysplasia can live normal lives.

Treatment

Dogs with this condition must not be allowed to become overweight as this will aggravate the condition. Dogs may be prescribed anti-inflammatory drugs like Rimadyl, which is also given to arthritic dogs. In severe cases, dogs with hip dysplasia may need hip replacements.

Summing Up

- Caring for a dog with special needs can be difficult at times, but ultimately it's very satisfying.

- Make sure you research your dog's condition well so you know what to do in the event of an emergency. There are lots of websites devoted to conditions affecting dogs and many will have great resources and tips on how to cope and make your dog's life fulfilling.

- Always check with your vet before you begin giving your dog any supplements – you don't know how it will react with regular medication or treatments.

Chapter Eleven

Adopting a Dog

There are so many dogs in the UK who have, for one reason or another, ended up with a rehoming charity. If you are thinking about getting a dog, why not look into a rescue dog?

Rescue centres

Sadly there is a huge stray and unwanted dog problem in the UK. If you have a particular type of breed in mind, there are charities that specialise in certain breeds, mainly because they are special types of dogs that need special handling, preferably in a home where the owners have experience of that breed.

Homes for older dogs are particularly in demand, this is because puppies are generally easier to find homes for.

The charities

Dogs Trust

Dogs Trust was founded in 1891 and formerly called the Canine Defence League. They boast of never putting a healthy dog down and have 17 rescue centres in the UK. They have also recently opened one in the Republic of Ireland. Dogs Trust care for around 16,000 dogs every single year, they also foster the dogs of those who are fleeing domestic violence and run various campaigns, including one to get landlords to rent accommodation to people with dogs.

You can view a list of dogs that need rehoming on their website and also find out all about how the rehoming process works.

My experience of Dogs Trust

In September 2009 my partner and I were devastated when our dog Vic died. We were sponsoring a dog with Dogs Trust, so that's where we turned when we decided it was time to get another dog.

Part of the adoption process with Dogs Trust is to do a walk past of the kennels and choose a dog you like the look of, my partner and I didn't feel comfortable doing that. When we went to Dogs Trust and explained this they were very understanding and instead went through their files to find a dog that we had a suitable home for. This was how we were paired with 17-month-old Benjy, a Labrador cross who had been with the centre since he was seven months old after his owners had lost their home. Benjy was described as a 'straightforward boy with no issues' by staff and within days he had settled into his new home.

Blue Cross

Blue Cross helps almost 100,000 animals a year through their adoption centres and animal hospitals. To view the animals that need rehoming go to their website, you can also find out about their adoption process there.

RSPCA

RSPCA is the oldest animal welfare organisation in the UK. In 2008 the RSPCA found homes for 70,017 animals. You can search on their website for animals that need a new home in your local area. Remember that many of these animals have been abused and need and deserve a good home.

The SSPCA are the Scottish version of the RSPCA but they're not the same organisation, and, if you live in Ireland there's the Dublin Society for the Prevention of Cruelty to Animals (see the help list for more details).

Battersea Dogs and Cats Home

Battersea Dogs and Cats Home has been established for 150 years. To adopt a dog from them the fee is £95 which includes microchipping and vaccinations. You can view animals in need of rehoming on their website and also find out about the adoption process.

List of rescue centres

The Dog Rescue Pages can be found at www.dogpages.org.uk. They feature all different breeds of dogs from rescue centres and private homes.

Special breed rescue centres

These are dogs needing a home with someone who has experience of whatever particular breed they deal with. Before you think of adopting one of these dogs, think long and hard about the responsibility taking on a special breed will entail, do some research and make a decision about whether you can make the commitment needed to provide a good home for one of these dogs.

Greyhounds

Greyhounds are great dogs for families. They are good with children and don't need much walking, but they do need plenty of room to stretch out in. However, greyhounds are not a good idea if you have any other small animals as they have been trained to chase anything small and furry.

The Retired Greyhound Trust can be found at www.retiredgreyhounds.co.uk. If you live in Ireland, visit www.dogrescueireland.com.

Rottweilers

Peter Beach, who has 32 years' experience of the breed, founded the Rottweiler Rescue Trust. Find them at www.rottweilerrescuetrust.co.uk. They have an abundance of advice on living with Rottweilers.

Staffordshire bull terriers

Staffies are actually a gentle breed of dog, hence their nickname 'the nanny dog'. Staffordshire Bull Terrier Rescue lists regional rehoming centres, go to www.sbtse.org.uk.

Big dogs

Big Dog Rescue work to rehome large and giant breeds – like bull mastiffs, Great Danes and German shepherds – in the UK. You can find them at http://bigdogrescue.org.uk.

How the adoption process works

No matter where you adopt a dog from, the process is generally the same:

'Rescue centres will be flexible.'

- You will complete a questionnaire either at the rehoming centre or online. It will ask you questions like 'do you own your own home?' and 'do you have an enclosed garden?' and other things about where you live. If you are a tenant you may be asked for written permission from your landlord that confirms they are agreeable to you keeping a pet. One of the main reasons for dogs being handed to rehoming centres is because tenants are forced to give up their pet.

- You'll get to meet staff at the rehoming centre who will try to match you with a dog to fit your lifestyle. This means, for example, they won't give a St Bernard to someone who lives in a flat or a Yorkshire terrier to someone used to bigger dogs.

- You'll get to see the dogs in the kennels, however, if you don't feel comfortable doing this you can explain to the staff – they'll come up with a list of dogs they think might suit you and your lifestyle. Usually the files will contain plenty of information, including things like whether the dog gets on with cats, whether he or she barks and why they ended up in the centre.

- You'll meet the dog and get to take them for a walk – often rehoming centres like you to visit the dog more than once.

- The rehoming centre staff will do a home visit to make sure your home is suitable. If you live a great distance away this may be done at the same time as they bring your chosen dog or before you go to collect them – ask the staff if this will be possible when you arrange everything.

- You'll get a pre-adoption talk to help you settle your new dog into your home and be given an adoption form to sign, this will detail your responsibilities towards your new best friend.

- A date will be set for you to take your new pet home or have them brought to you. You can pay the fee (if applicable) for the adoption there and then or when you collect your new dog. Fees will vary, e.g. Dogs Trust charge £80-£100, the RSPCA £90 for dogs and puppies. All dogs in the care of Dogs Trust and RSPCA are neutered or spayed and microchipped. If that hasn't been done yet you may be asked to bring your dog back to get it done or given a letter to take to your vet.

- Your new dog will get a full health check to make sure they're in tip top condition. If they have an existing medical condition the rehoming centre will usually pay for treatment.

- Afterwards you can contact the rehoming centre for help or advice. There's often a clause in the adoption contract saying that if for whatever reason you no longer want your dog you must return them to the rehoming centre you got them from.

Be aware that if you have children or other pets they will need to be introduced to your chosen dog before you are allowed to adopt.

The myths about dog adoption

- 'You don't know what you are getting' – this suggests that if you adopt a dog you may unwittingly end up with one that has a hidden history of aggression. Most dog charities will check the temperament of dogs who end up in their care and make you aware of any problems or potential problems that might come up. The last thing they want is for dogs to be returned.

- 'You'll be lumbered with a big vet's bill' – in most cases the dogs are fit and well. In cases where they're not, the rescue centre will often pay for the treatment your pet needs, however, you should check this with them. In any case, they will make you aware of any treatment the dog has received while in their care.

- 'You can't take the dog back' – If things don't work out you can.

- 'It's expensive' – this is not the case. Many puppies or dogs will cost hundreds of pounds if you buy them – a rehoming centre will ask for a donation or fee usually around £100 so it actually works out cheaper in most cases.

- 'There must be something wrong with the dogs because they end up in the rehoming centre' – there are many reasons why perfectly good dogs end up in rescue homes, the rehoming centre will be able to tell you the circumstances regarding why each dog has been brought in.

- 'Dogs from abusive homes can never make good pets' – with love and attention and the right training, no matter what a dog has been through they can live a happy and normal life. Dogs quickly adapt to their new life and that includes getting plenty of love from you. However, some dogs from abusive homes can need experienced owners, the rehoming centre will take your experience and the dog's background into account before allowing you to adopt.

Summing Up

▪ There are many charities that have been rehoming dogs and other animals for years. They are experienced in pairing the right dog to the right owners and will ensure that you are adopting a dog suited to your home, lifestyle and experience.

▪ There are also rehoming centres for specific breeds, these breeds are usually dogs that are special in some way, e.g. ex-racing greyhounds.

▪ The adoption process is very detailed and aims to pair the right dog with the right owner – the last thing a rehoming centre wants is dogs being returned because people don't have the time or space once they've taken a dog home!

▪ You will have to pay or make a donation to the rehoming centre for the dog you are adopting – check the fees with them when you initially contact them.

▪ Bear in mind that many dogs end up in rehoming centres often for purely unfortunate circumstances and not because they are 'damaged' in any way.

Help List

Animal Cancer Trust

5 Flag Business Exchange, Vicarage Farm Road, Peterborough, Cambs, PE1 5TX
Tel: 08701 644 225
info@animalcancertrust.org.uk
www.animalcancertrust.org.uk
Aims to provide education and information that helps owners and veterinary
surgeons understand more about cancer and what treatments are possible.

Animal Passports

www.animalpassports.co.uk
Find out about where your pet is eligible to travel on this website.

Association of Pet Dog Trainers (APDT)

PO Box 17, Kempsford, GL7 4WZ
Tel: 01285 810 811
APDToffice@aol.com
www.apdt.co.uk
Offers pet owners a guarantee of quality when looking for a training class or
a puppy class in their area. All members of the APDT have been assessed
according to a Code of Practice. There is a search facility so you can find dog
trainers in your local area.

BARF World

www.barfworld.com
Information on the BARF diet can be found on this website.

Battersea Dogs and Cats Home

www.battersea.org.uk
Battersea Dogs and Cats Home reunite lost dogs and cats with their owners;
and when they can't do this, they care for them until new homes can be found.
See the website for details of animals currently needing a new home.

Big Dog Rescue

http://bigdogrescue.org.uk
Aims to rehome most breeds of large and giant dogs to loving homes in the uk.

Blue Cross

Shilton Road, Burford, Oxon, OX18 4PF
Tel: 01993 822651
info@bluecross.org.uk
www.bluecross.org.uk
Provides a service meeting all the welfare needs of companion animals through treatment, advice and support, and finding them caring homes. Check the website for rehoming centres near you.

Canine Epilepsy

www.canineepilepsy.co.uk
Website contains information on canine epilepsy for both veterinary surgeons and owners of dogs that have been diagnosed with epilepsy.

Canine Epilepsy Guardian Angels

www.canine-epilepsy-guardian-angels.com
Provides information on canine epilepsy and other diseases

Canine Epilepsy Support Group

Westholme, 21 Sea Lane, East Preston, Littlehampton, West Sussex, BN16 1NH
Tel: 01903 784 263 (helpline)
www.canineepilepsysupport.co.uk
Offers practical and sympathetic support to the owners of epileptic pets, and the opportunity to talk to people who have learnt to live happily with an epileptic pet.

Ciao.co.uk

www.ciao.co.uk
Website full of consumer reviews, search pet insurance to see what people have to say about the policies available.

Compare the Market

www.comparethemarket.com
Comparison website where you can compare pet insurance.

Confused.com

www.confused.com
Comparison website where you can compare pet insurance.

Deaf Dal

www.deafdal.co.uk
A website dedicated to Humphrey the deaf Dalmatian. The site includes information on hand signs, good books to read on the subject, training tips and links to other websites.

Department of Agriculture, Fisheries and Food (Ireland)

Tel: 1890 505 604 (helpline)
pets@agriculture.gov.ie
www.agriculture.gov.ie
Visit the Department of Agriculture, Fisheries and Food for information on the pet passport scheme in Ireland.

Department of Environment, Food and Rural Affairs (DEFRA)

Tel: 0870 2411 710 (helpline, Monday to Friday, 8am-6pm)
quarantine@animalhealth.gsi.gov.uk
www.defra.gov.uk
Visit DEFRA's website for information on pet passports and the Pet Travel Scheme.

Direct Line

www.directline.com
Check the website for details of pet insurance available.

Dog-Friendly Britain

www.dogfriendlybritain.co.uk
Information on dog-friendly holidays and days out can be found here.

DogsLost

www.doglost.co.uk
DogLost is a national network of thousands of dog owners and volunteers, keen to help reunite lost dogs with their owners.

Dogs Invited

www.dogsinvited.co.uk
Information on dog-friendly accommodation in the UK.

Dog People

www.dogpeople.co.uk
A directory of pet-friendly accommodation and dog-friendly hotels, self-catering, cottages, B&Bs, pubs, places to eat, attractions and holiday parks within the UK.

Dog Rescue Ireland

www.dogrescueireland.com
Charity dedicated to rescuing and rehoming unwanted, abandoned Irish greyhounds and dogs.

Dog Rescue Pages

www.dogpages.org.uk
An entirely non-commercial website which aims to encourage more people to consider adopting one of the many thousands of dogs waiting for new homes in rescue centres and shelters throughout the UK and Ireland.

Dogs Trust

17 Wakely Street, London, EC1 7RQ
Tel: 0207 837 0006
www.dogstrust.org.uk
The largest dog welfare charity in the UK. Visit their website to search for a rescue centre near you, you can also find the rehoming questionnaires and information on the rehoming process on their website.

Dogs Trust (Ireland)

Ashbourne Road, Finglas, Dublin 11
Tel: 1890 252 928
enquiries@dogstrust.ie
www.dogstrust.ie
Dogs Trust in Ireland opened its first rehoming centre in October 2009. Visit their website to view dogs that need new homes and for information on the rehoming criteria they look for.

Dorwest Herbs

www.dorwest.com
The leading authority on veterinary herbal medicine, the website has an A-Z of common problems and a frequently asked questions section.

Dublin SPCA

www.dspca.ie
Charity fighting animal cruelty and abuse in all of its forms. See the website for animals needing a new home.

Endangered Dogs Defence and Rescue (EDDR)

PO Box 1544, London, W7 2ZB
Tel: 07020 934072 (helpline)
doglaw@endangereddogs.com
www.endangereddogs.com
A voluntary run organisation offering free information, education and advice to help, defend and better protect dogs in need. They give advice concerning dog-related legal matters and legislation affecting dogs.

Eurotunnel

www.eurotunnel.com
Find information about travelling with your pet on the Eurotunnel.

Frontline

http://frontline.uk.merial.com
Frontline is considered the best treatment by vets for dogs who have fleas and or ticks. The website includes a stockist and vet finder.

Go Compare

www.gocompare.com

Comparison website where you can search for pet insurance policies.

Kong Company

www.kongcompany.com

A brand of dog toy in which you can hide treats for your dog.

National Pet Register

www.nationalpetregister.org

A database of missing pets checked by police, vets and animal shelters.

PDSA

Tel: 0800 731 2502

www.pdsa.org.uk

Cares for the pets of people in need. They provide veterinary services to their sick and injured animals and promote responsible pet ownership.

Pets Get Slim

www.petsgetslim.co.uk

RSPCA website dedicated to helping pets lose weight.

Pet Holidays

www.petholidays.com

Website which provides guides to pet-friendly holidays in the UK.

Pet Insurance Online

www.petinsuranceonline.co.uk

Compare the latest pet insurance offers, quotes and news from the UK's top insurers.

Petplan

www.petplan.co.uk

Specialise in pet insurance and are recommended by Dogs Trust.

Retired Greyhound Trust

www.retiredgreyhounds.co.uk
Charity dedicated to rehoming ex-racing greyhounds. Visit the website for information on centres local to you.

Rottweiler Rescue Trust

www.rottweilerrescuetrust.co.uk
A charity dedicated to rescuing and rehoming Rottweilers.

RSPCA

Wilberforce Way, Southwater, Horsham, West Sussex, RH13 9RS
Tel: 0300 1234 555 (infoline)
www.rspca.org.uk
The leading animal welfare charity. You can search for your local rehoming centre on the website.

SSPCA

Kingseat Road, Halbeath, Dunfermline , KY11 8RY
Tel: 03000 999999 (helpline)
www.scottishspca.org
Scotland's animal welfare charity. The SSPCA's objectives are to prevent cruelty to animals and encourage kindness and humanity in their treatment. You can find information on local rehoming centres on the website.

Staffordshire Bull Terrier Welfare

www.sbtse.org.uk
Charity dedicated to rescuing and rehoming Staffies.

Vetbase

www.vetbase.co.uk
Useful information on animal health can be found on this website.

Book List

Complete Idiot's Guide to Positive Dog Training
By Pamela Dennison, Penguin, USA, 2006.

The Dog Whisperer: The Compassionate, Nonviolent Approach to Dog Training
By Paul Owens and Norma Eckroate, Adams Media Corporation, USA, 2007.

Hear, Hear! A Guide to Training a Deaf Dog
By Barry Eaton, self-published, 2005

Living with Blind Dogs
By Caroline D Levin, Lantern Books, USA, 2008.

Need - 2 - Know

Available Titles Include ...

Allergies A Parent's Guide
ISBN 978-1-86144-064-8 £8.99

Autism A Parent's Guide
ISBN 978-1-86144-069-3 £8.99

Drugs A Parent's Guide
ISBN 978-1-86144-043-3 £8.99

Dyslexia and Other Learning Difficulties
A Parent's Guide ISBN 978-1-86144-042-6 £8.99

Bullying A Parent's Guide
ISBN 978-1-86144-044-0 £8.99

Epilepsy The Essential Guide
ISBN 978-1-86144-063-1 £8.99

Teenage Pregnancy The Essential Guide
ISBN 978-1-86144-046-4 £8.99

Gap Years The Essential Guide
ISBN 978-1-86144-079-2 £8.99

How to Pass Exams A Parent's Guide
ISBN 978-1-86144-047-1 £8.99

Child Obesity A Parent's Guide
ISBN 978-1-86144-049-5 £8.99

Applying to University The Essential Guide
ISBN 978-1-86144-052-5 £8.99

ADHD The Essential Guide
ISBN 978-1-86144-060-0 £8.99

Student Cookbook - Healthy Eating The Essential Guide
ISBN 978-1-86144-061-7 £8.99

Stress The Essential Guide
ISBN 978-1-86144-054-9 £8.99

Adoption and Fostering A Parent's Guide
ISBN 978-1-86144-056-3 £8.99

Special Educational Needs A Parent's Guide
ISBN 978-1-86144-057-0 £8.99

The Pill An Essential Guide
ISBN 978-1-86144-058-7 £8.99

University A Survival Guide
ISBN 978-1-86144-072-3 £8.99

Diabetes The Essential Guide
ISBN 978-1-86144-059-4 £8.99

View the full range at **www.need2knowbooks.co.uk**. To order our titles,
call **01733 898103**, email **sales@n2kbooks.com** or visit the website.

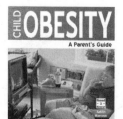  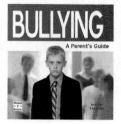  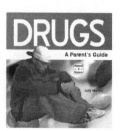

Need - 2 - Know, Remus House, Coltsfoot Drive, Peterborough, PE2 9JX